The Gates Shall Not

"And I say also unto thee,
That thou art Peter, and
upon this rock I will
build my church; and the
gates of hell shall not
prevail against it"
(Matthew 16:18).

The Gates Shall Not

by
E. E. Cleveland

Review and Herald Publishing Association
Nashville, TN   Washington, DC

Copyright © 1981 by
Review and Herald Publishing Association
Published in Nashville, Tennessee

This book was
Designed by Dean Tucker

Type set: 10/12 Century Schoolbook
Printed in U.S.A.

Library of Congress Cataloging in Publication Data

Cleveland, Edward Earl.
    The gates shall not.

    1. Seventh-day Adventists—Doctrinal and controversial works.
I. Title.
BX6154.C54   230'.67   80-27033
ISBN 0-8127-0325-1

Contents

Introduction

The writer does not intend to tie the thirteen chapters of this book to the specific chapters of the Sabbath School lessons being studied at this time. Rather, he wishes to provide the reader with a panoramic view of the exodus of God's children from modern Egypt to the Promised Land. This story has been told and retold in other works. It is, however, the author's burden that by providing this work, with compact chapters, the time-conscious businessman will read it through. The author further hopes that the doctrinal connotations will make this book a missionary tool for the ardent soul winner.

The Seventh-day Adventist Church stands solidly on the preachments of Scripture. I am continually aware of this as in evangelism I witness firsthand the anointing of the Holy Spirit as I preach. At this writing I am in the eighth week of an evangelistic campaign, preaching seven nights weekly. Hundreds still press eagerly in night after night to hear the Word of God. The Advent message has lost none of its truthfulness or power.

May the reader of this book find inspiration to become a communicant of the faith. With this, I shall rest satisfied.

E. E. Cleveland

Chapter 1

The Church

Adam's sin had many unpleasant consequences. Among them were sickness, death, war, social discord, famine, and destructive manifestations in nature. But it is also responsible for one blessing of global import: It alone provided a reason for the existence of the church. The church—*ekklēsia*—is a Christian body of "called out ones." We are called out of the sin into which our father Adam plunged us.

The original seduction of man concerned Heaven long before the creation of Adam. Scripture clearly indicates this. "Forasmuch as ye know that ye were not redeemed with corruptible things, as silver and gold, from your vain conversation received by tradition from your fathers; but with the precious blood of Christ, as of a lamb without blemish and without spot: who verily was foreordained before the foundation of the world, but was manifest in these last times for you" (1 Peter 1:18-20). God the Father entered into a painful agreement that would make possible the redemption of man.

"I saw the lovely Jesus, and beheld an expression of sympathy and sorrow upon his countenance. Soon I saw him approach the exceeding bright light which enshrouded the Father. . . . The anxiety of the angels seemed to be intense while Jesus was communing with his Father. Three times he was shut in by the glorious

9

light about the Father, and the third time he came from the Father, his person could be seen. His countenance was calm, free from all perplexity and trouble, and shone with benevolence and loveliness, such as words cannot express. He then made known to the angelic host that a way of escape had been made for lost man. . . . Jesus told them that he would stand between the wrath of his Father and guilty man, that he would bear iniquity and scorn, and but few would receive him as the Son of God" (*Spiritual Gifts,* Vol. I, pp. 23, 24).

Thus, before the creation of man, God prepared for the emergency. By so doing, God did not foreordain that man should fall, but He certainly prepared for the eventuality. His preparation for man's future testifies to His wisdom. Such an acknowledgment is not a statement of complicity. Had God dictated the future of man, He would have programmed him not to sin. But this would have robbed man of his freedom—his power to choose—and thus his capacity for happiness.

When Adam sinned, God faced three courses of action: (1) He could destroy man from the planet. (2) He could change the law that man had transgressed. (3) Or He could assume responsibility for man's failure, pay the penalty for his guilt, and open a door of hope for his redemption.

God refused to destroy man. He loved him too much to do this without giving man an opportunity to be saved. Such divine love is beyond human comprehension, for to spare man, Jesus Himself must die. God's love for man was pitted against His love for Himself! It occasioned the real agony of divine decision-making. What mysterious essence characterizes God's love, we cannot know. But of this we are certain: The visible evidences of that love are unmistakable. The manger,

Jesus' life of unselfish service, the cross, the tomb—all reveal God's love. "But God commendeth his love toward us, in that, while we were yet sinners, Christ died for us" (Romans 5:8).

In consequence of Adam's fall, would God change His law to justify man? Such a course would spell disaster, for it would necessitate changing God's law every time man sinned. Soon the moral law would, indeed, become a shadow. Heaven decided against this course of action. "My covenant will I not break, nor alter the thing that is gone out of my lips" (Psalm 89:34).

It was the third alternative that brought to this earth Heaven's choicest gift. The covenant that made this possible was mysterious in its process and import. God the Father and God the Son agreed that Christ would take man's place before God's offended law. He would bear the consequence of man's transgression. We cannot explain Their painful decision. Scripture calls it the "mystery of godliness" (1 Timothy 3:16).

For nearly four thousand years pen and voice heralded the coming Messiah. The sacrificial system, instituted after sin, prefigured the coming Christ. The shedding of the innocent blood of animals promised a more excellent sacrifice to come. Christ would appear on earth in human flesh, endure thirty-three years of painful human relationships, and die as a man for the sins of the world. "He veiled His divinity with the garb of humanity and appeared mysteriously in a manger as the son of Mary. In His life and death, He would furnish the harshest skeptic with proof that could not be contradicted of His love for man."

The atonement would make possible for man an adjustment in position, condition, and ultimately environment. God would, by giving Himself, open a door of hope for all mankind.

He commissioned the Old Testament church to carry the Good News of the coming Christ to an ignorant world. This they failed to do. Instead, they hoarded the blessings and shut themselves off spiritually from the outside world. Jehovah became "the God of the Hebrews" instead of "the God of the world." They prided themselves in their rituals and temple. No Gentile shadow was allowed to fall in the temple precincts. "Hear, O Israel: The Lord our God is one Lord" became a call of the Jews, by the Jews, and for the Jews. The Judeo-church movement stalemated. Clearly "the fulness of the time" had come.

Into the world Jesus came—a startling development that would affect mankind at every level of existence. He would condemn the Jewish church as self-centered, ritual-oriented, and image-conscious. It was a drifting ship—without chart or compass—on a shoreless sea. He would build a church, with Himself the foundation, against which "the gates of hell" would not prevail. He would demonstrate in word and deed what life at its best is all about. He would at last be crucified for the sins of the world, "wounded for our transgressions, . . . bruised for our iniquities" (Isaiah 53:5). But He would rise and ascend to God. There He would judge the quick and the dead. Thereafter He would come again to receive His waiting church. And both He and it will at last be satisfied.

Chapter 2

The First-Century Church

In His parting counsel Christ sought to reassure the fledgling church that it would succeed. "Nevertheless I tell you the truth; It is expedient for you that I go away: for if I go not away, the Comforter will not come unto you; but if I depart, I will send him unto you" (John 16:7). Few in number and under fire from secular and religious authorities, the church faced an uncertain future. Speaking to this need, Christ promised: "Ye shall receive power, after that the Holy Ghost is come upon you: and ye shall be witnesses unto me" (Acts 1:8). Jesus' promise quickened the pulse of His eager listeners. He was not leaving them alone to compete with evil men and demons. Though Christ Himself must leave, His Replacement would be adequate for both the mission and the emergencies of the church in all ages.

The very nature of the church predestines it to persecution. It is otherworldly at its heart. As with its Founder, there are basic incompatibilities that cannot be harmonized. The church must change the world, or the world will change the church. One or the other will destroy the other. In short, when Jesus planted His church here, the seeds of church-world conflict were sown. Some read of the pagan persecutions of Christians in the first century, and they are puzzled that the church has had to suffer so. The answer lies here: Human governments have wandered so far from God's will that they view the church as subversive to the unity of any dictatorial nation. Only in those countries that practice democratic principles does the church have complete freedom of action. Christianity is an absolute system that requires its followers to seek "first the kingdom of God, and his righteousness" (Matthew 6:33). To make God first is intolerable for some governmental systems. Hence, persecution. Ultimately, the God of the church will triumph over His enemies. But for now He tests His followers' allegiance by fire and sword. "Must Jesus bear the cross alone, And all the world go free? No, there's a cross for every one, And there's a cross for me."

Accompanied by a cloud of angels, Christ ascended to heaven. There He began a work of grace for His followers that includes intercession, mediation, substitution, and judgment.

His disciples repaired to the privacy of an upper room to await the coming of the Comforter. "And when the day of Pentecost was fully come, they were all with one accord in one place. And suddenly there came a sound from heaven as of a rushing mighty wind, and it filled all the house where they were sitting. . . . And they were all filled with the Holy Ghost, and began to speak with other tongues, as the Spirit gave them utterance" (Acts 2:1-4).

The Comforter had, indeed, come. And His coming had been signaled by a multilingual demonstration that clearly indicated its divine origin. Representatives of seventeen nations and territories heard the gospel in their own languages from the lips of men unschooled in these tongues. The gift of tongues was exhibited again and again in the experiences of new converts. It certified that Christ had sent the Holy Spirit to continue His work on a broader scale.

God gave the gift of tongues for purposes of communication, and as such it will be manifest from time to time as the Holy Spirit deems necessary. But as a sign of the coming of the Comforter, tongues shall cease (1 Corinthians 13:8). And, indeed, they have ceased to be a sign of the coming of the Comforter. We now have the written record of Acts. There no longer exists any necessity to establish the Spirit's coming by signs and wonders. Now we need only read the record of Acts and receive personally the presence of the Holy Spirit in our lives.

The baptism of the Holy Spirit made a basic difference in the lives of the disciples. From fear-ridden preachers cowering in a locked room they became bold proclaimers of the faith: "Now when they saw the boldness of Peter and John, and perceived that they were unlearned and ignorant men, they marvelled; and they took knowledge of them, that they had been with Jesus" (Acts 4:13).

Thomas carried the gospel to India. John endured banishment for the faith. James was beheaded, and Peter was crucified. Martyrdom became a way of life for many during the next ten centuries. The spirit of the early church was best expressed in the words of the apostle: "Whether it be right in the sight of God to hearken unto you more than unto God, judge ye. For we cannot but speak the things which we have seen and heard" (verses 19, 20).

The church was put on the earth to preach the gospel. It may engage in other enterprises, but it is at its best when it serves the supreme purpose of its existence. Accordingly, all of the apostles were preachers. This is significant. The original church was a congregation of preachers. There were no exceptions. Small wonder that the church affected the known world so dramatically that the disciples were said to have "turned the world upside down" (Acts 17:6).

Every-member involvement was the key to the rapid

growth of the church body. And it will be so in the end of the age. In God's sight every convert is a convert-maker. The first-century church did not do its best work through a vested clergy, though it had one. The fifteenth chapter of Acts indicates this. But the church did not rely on clergy for the propagation of the faith. Men, women, and children joined in the grand enterprise. "And the word of God increased; and the number of the disciples multiplied in Jerusalem greatly; and a great company of the priests were obedient to the faith" (Acts 6:7).

But it was the purpose of Jehovah that all men be exposed to the Good News. Shortsighted Christians have not always understood this. God has often had to allow evil men to hedge up the way, leaving Christians no alternative but to branch out into unentered areas. This was the case with the early church. "When the Jews saw the multitudes, they were filled with envy, and spake against those things which were spoken by Paul, contradicting and blaspheming. Then Paul and Barnabas waxed bold, and said, It was necessary that the word of God should first have been spoken to you: but seeing ye put it from you, and judge yourselves unworthy of everlasting life, lo, we turn to the Gentiles" (Acts 13:45, 46). Never were more appropriate words employed to express the ultimate purposes of God in this regard. "For so hath the Lord commanded us, saying, I have set thee to be a light of the Gentiles, that thou shouldest be for salvation unto the ends of the earth" (verse 47).

The church in its mission was urged on to active conquest of the unsaved. The church is pastoral and evangelistic in nature. Scripture does not picture the church as a citadel of God on a sea of evil. Rather, it is like yeast, aggressively altering all that it touches. The idea of evangelism disturbs some church members. Church boards have been known to vote against evangelistic meetings. Such thinking would make the church an army of occupation. But the spirit of the gospel commission precludes this limitation of goals. The church exists for evangelism. This was the spirit of the first-century church. And thus it must ever be!

Two cardinal doctrines form the crux of the apostles' messages: the lordship of Jesus Christ and the binding claims of His holy law. Again and again these cardinal themes appear. It was to be and is the basis of church unity worldwide. The city or country cannot affect this. The church is *one* if it retains these essential features. The presence of the Holy Spirit achieves the unity of the believers. But the twin doctrines of the lordship of Christ and the perpetuity and relevance of divine law form the basis of global understanding.

It must be understood that when Jesus ascended, He was by no means universally accepted as the Son of God. The New Testament preachers had to hammer home the truth of His divinity again and again. It was and is the foundation stone of the Christian faith, as attested to by John (John 1:1, 4, 14), Peter (Acts 2:36), and Paul (Acts 9:20).

Jesus is the Life Substance of the church. Without Him Christianity has no drawing power. He is the central theme of every effective sermon. He is the theme of every meaningful religious discussion. He is praised in hymn and prayer. He is the Light of the church and of the world. "In him was life; and the life was the light of men" (John 1:4). The church exists to advertise Jesus.

And, of course, there is the law. Paul declared it to be "holy, and just, and good" (Romans 7:12). It is the foundation of justice throughout the universe. It is perpetual and applicable to all aspects of life. The apostles never even hinted that the law of God was dispensational. They proclaimed it as the verbalized will of God in capsule form. Jesus Himself upheld the law as the transcript of His own character. He declared emphatically that it is perpetual (Matthew 5:17-19). Paul insisted the importance of the law in Romans 7:12. James affirmed it in James 2:10-12. And the apostle John pointed to this same cardinal truth in John 14:15.

And so the church of God grew. To Corinth, Thessalonica, Colosse, Galatia, Ephesus, Smyrna, Laodicea, and farther the gospel spread. The early church did not splinter when it obeyed the same gospel. (See Philippians 3:16 and 1 Corinthians 1:10.)And today's Babylonian religious spectrum stands rebuked in the light of that unity. The present confusion in the church is not of divine origin. In the next chapter we will deal with this.

Chapter 3

A House Divided

"For I know this, that after my departing shall grievous wolves enter in among you, not sparing the flock. Also of your own selves shall men arise, speaking perverse things, to draw away disciples after them" (Acts 20:29, 30). Paul here spoke of division in the house of God. And he predicted that the attack on the church would come from within and without. The unity known during the Pentecostal experience would soon be shattered. And the initial pressures were external.

The Christian church had its birth during the reign of the Caesars. Some of these dictators regarded the church as dangerous to the interests of the empire. Nero, Domitian, Trajan, Marcus Aurelius, Commodus, Diocletian, and others did their bloody work on history's center stage. So fierce was their work of death that the streets of Rome ran red with blood, and burning Christians lighted the grounds of the Circus Maximus. But in all of this, Christians went willingly to the chopping block or to the stake. These emperors may have tried to extinguish the light of truth, but instead the influence of Christianity reached even into their households.

The pressures on the church seem to have been felt first and fiercest at Rome, the capital of the world empire. Some of the emperors viewed the existence of the hated sect as an affront to their authority. Concerted efforts were sporadically put forth to exterminate the Christian church. Christianity was eventually outlawed in the empire, and the anguish of the saints began. Blood relatives turned against their own families to curry favor with civil officials. Informers covered the saints with calumny, charging them with the most bestial of crimes and practices. Because of the nature of the Communion Service, enemies accused Christians of cannibalism. Their worship of God was regarded as disrespect of the emperor. Refusal to pour a libation to the emperor meant certain death.

Stirring scenes of rare, raw courage grace the pages of the history of those times. In their martyrdoms Polycarp—Bishop of Smyrna—and Blandina of the Ephesians and countless others covered themselves with glory. "They loved not their lives," but rather they cheerfully sacrificed themselves for the Master's sake. Christ was thus honored by their sacrifices.

Two absolute systems had collided and left no room for compromise. Christ had said, "The gates of hell shall not prevail against . . . [the church]" (Matthew 16:18). As a result the church triumphed, whereas the Roman Empire disintegrated. The mad emperors would become only a painful memory. Secular historians might glorify the death-dealing deeds of warriors and the glittering facade of culture and philosophy. But in the Roman Empire the right of dissent was not always known, and tolerance sometimes became a forgotten word.

During this time of persecution the bishops of Rome made a fatal decision. In the interest of "saving the church" they reasoned that they must assuage the anger of the emperor. So they surrendered some of the church's distinctive doctrines. But to erase the line of demarcation between the church and the world would, if successful, surrender peacefully to the enemy that which he could not take by force.

As the church began to modify its doctrines it began to experience greater favor. Its adoption of Sunday as a day of worship brought many influential heathen into its ranks. Since Sunday was a pagan holiday, its adoption by the church made its members less conspicuous. Persecution of the Roman Church eased somewhat. Encouraged, the Roman church fathers went a step further. They introduced images into church worship. Other compromises followed in rapid succession. Christening replaced immersion. The mediation of Mary and of an endless succession of saints further paganized the Roman Church. Each doctrinal defection further ingratiated the Roman Church with the state. Persecution finally ceased in Rome altogether. Ultimately the church enlisted the power of the state to strengthen its influence.

Turning east, then west, and south, what the persuasion of priests failed to do, the armies accomplished. But it was not easy. In fact, it was a bloody work. The pages of history have faithfully recorded the cruelties practiced in the name of Christ. In Ethiopia, where the Coptic faith held sway and the true Sabbath was observed, even military pressure failed to rob them of their allegiance to the true day of worship. Though the Ethiopians were forced to accept the pagan Sunday, they nevertheless clung to the day observed by their fathers for centuries.

In Europe dissenters simply went underground. Dissent from the doctrinal deviations of Rome was more stubborn and widespread than is generally known. The Albigenses, Waldenses, and others wrote their tales of heroism in their resistance movements. Physical warfare accompanied the Roman effort to subdue these dissidents, but the geography of their dwelling places helped them immeasurably. The difficult terrain made resistance easier for the light bearers.

They were a simple but earnest people. With portions of God's Word concealed on their persons, they would venture into the cities. They would teach truth wherever they could find a listening ear. Thus the Word of God was spread in spite of the vigilance of priests and soldiers. Members of some families betrayed their loved ones. Christians were burned, put on torture racks, thrown to wild beasts, and stretched on revolving wheels until every joint was strained. Every form of torture that fiendish minds could concoct was employed in the effort to extend Romanism by compelling the conscience.

The Catholic Church extended its influence over the arts, sciences, and government. Freedom to experiment and draw conclusions was subject to the decision of church councils. Due to priestly meddling, Galileo had to meekly subordinate his correct conclusion that the earth is round to the erroneous view that it was flat. Most of the art of the Middle Ages was religion-oriented. Michelangelo and Raphael were lionized by the prelates for their priceless work, which was Bible-oriented. Many kings, princes, and governors ruled with the permission of the pontiffs. To dramatize this fact, one temporal ruler had to stand in the snow outside of the pope's residence for hours before being admitted.

But such control could not last forever. Two events broke the stranglehold of centuries on the life of the world: the Renaissance and the Reformation.

In art, philosophy, and the sciences intellectuals began breaking the shackles of centuries. Painting, which had been largely confined to religious themes, now embraced all phases of the human life-style. There were remarkable breakthroughs in science as it related to transportation, medicine, and diet. Scholars began reviving the ancient languages of Hebrew and Greek.

Meanwhile, the Reformation began in Europe, and it

could not be denied. John Huss of Bohemia paid with his
life for his faith, but others quickly rose to take his place.
Most notable was a Roman Catholic monk named Martin
Luther. His voice rose with the force of thunder in protest
against the excesses of the church. He wanted to reform
the church from within. He did not wish to start a new
movement. But the violence of hierarchal reaction to
him—excommunication—led to the formation of the Lutheran Church. However, Luther's influence extended
beyond denominational bounds. He was, in a sense, the
spark plug of the Reformation. His defense before the
Electors of Saxony at the Diet of Worms electrified the
world. His "kidnapping" and subsequent seclusion made
possible his translation of the Bible into the German
language. Other giants also arose to carry on. Calvin,
Tyndale, Melanchthon, and others extended the influence of the faith.

Toward the end of the eighteenth century, the French
Revolution broke out. The wide gap between the financial
"haves and have nots" had long before widened to the
point of breaking. The excesses of the French kings and
their courtiers were also a contributing factor to the revolution. The oppressive power of the clergy led to a rebellion against religion.

The guillotine worked overtime as militants tried to
supplant Catholicism. "Liberty, equality, fraternity" became the spiritual chant of the New France. French gen-
eral Berthier imprisoned the pope, bringing to an end
1260 years of papal domination. During the excesses that
accompanied the revolution, a French prostitute was carried down the avenues of Paris while the crowds chanted,
"Long live the Goddess of Reason."

Napoleon Bonaparte emerged from the political anar-
chy and became emperor of the New Republic. His constitution formed the foundation of law and order in all

democratic governments to follow. The political atmosphere changed, making possible freedom of religion and scientific research for experimentation.

To the west a new nation was emerging with principles of brotherhood written into its constitution. Civil and religious liberty would form the cornerstone of its political structure. More importantly, this land would become the home base of a Protestant missionary movement. Who could know then that the United States would become wealthy beyond belief and the economic backbone of the new religious thrust? Soon the Civil War would settle the slave question, and this new nation would thenceforth find little to disturb its institutional growth for years to come. And furthermore, with its isolation from the European continent, age-old conflicts no longer disturbed civilization. Thus, for two hundred years the Christian church has flourished in the United States, and from its shores missionaries have gone to the ends of the earth.

Chapter 4

The Protestant Dilemma

With the decline of papal influence, Protestantism spread like fire in stubble. "The Bible, and the Bible only, is our rule of faith," the protesters proclaimed. "Tradition is not equal in authority with Scripture," they said. But their most shocking conclusion was: A man may himself judge what is truth from a personal, prayerful study of the Scriptures. That the Holy Spirit speaks not alone to and through church councils went right to the heart of papal theology. The Reformers further insisted that Christ alone stands as Mediator between God and man. Man is saved solely on the merits of Christ's sacrifice for sin. The Reformation doctrine of free grace cut considerably into papal revenue. Divine providence had opened the door to freedom of religion. Centuries would pass before it could close again, if ever.

Wycliffe, Huss, Jerome, Zwingli, Luther, Tyndale, Calvin, and others laid the foundation for Protestantism that followed. Later the Wesley brothers in England forged a movement that has blessed the world. Roger Williams pioneered in the spread of the Protestant ethic. Human freedom, worldwide, was a direct response to the rise of Protestantism. The Protestant doctrine of the value of man sparked the various antislavery movements that arose so that one of the by-products of the Reformation was the liberation of the slaves. But beyond that, the doctrine of the separation of church and state received its birth.

It is important here to note that the Protestant dilemma surfaced early. Many of the tenets of Catholicism were never abandoned by the Reformers themselves. For this reason the traditional reform movements failed to continue their progress.

One of the ironies of Christendom is that it has persecuted in the name of Christ. Protestants suffered much at the hands of a church-dominated state. And some Protestant leaders persecuted dissidents within their ranks. It would seem that such intolerance would be immediately discarded. But this was not the case. Oliver Cromwell said it better than I ever could: "Is it ingenuous to ask liberty and not give it? What greater hypocrisy for those who were oppressed by the Bishop to become the oppressors themselves so soon as their yoke was removed?"

But this has ever been the case. Did not the oppressed Jews appeal to Roman authority to crucify Christ? It is difficult in our search of history to find a major religious power that did not try to enforce its beliefs. Martin Luther wrote to two friends in AD 1530: " 'I am pleased that you intend to publish a book against the Anabaptists as soon as possible. Since they are not only blasphemous, but also seditious men, let the sword exercise its rights over them, for it is the will of God that he shall have judgment who resisteth the power.'

"Melanchthon, . . . in a letter to the diet at Hamburg, in 1537, advocated death by the sword to all who professed Anabaptist views. Zwingli, the Swiss Reformer, who perished with the sword, and whose statue in Zürich pictures him with a Bible in his right hand and a sword in his left, persecuted not only the Baptists, but all dissenting sects who disagreed with his views. Even John Robinson, the renowned pastor of the Pilgrims in Holland, . . .

vigorously defended the use of the magistrate's power in matters of church discipline" (Charles S. Longacre, *Roger Williams,* p. 96). John Calvin shared these views.

The Pilgrims and the Puritans came to America in search of religious freedom, but they set up a system that did in the New World what the Papacy did in Europe. At issue was the question, "Should the state have and exercise authority in the enforcement of the first table of the Decalogue?" The Pilgrims and Puritans said "Yes" and proceeded to set up governments that would do the same. Dissenters were fined, placed in stocks, imprisoned, and in some instances put to death for disagreeing with the established order. So the United States began with the same weakness that its founders had come here to escape. Only the identity of the persecutor had changed. Persecution and its so-called justification remained.

Into this caldron came Roger Williams, a genuine free spirit. He had received his orientation in freedom-thinking in England under Sir Edward Coke, a great English jurist. When he arrived in America, Williams turned down the pastorate of Boston's most prestigious church because of the persecution policies of the Puritans. He accepted a pastorate in Salem, Massachusetts, but he was eventually hounded out of there by the Puritan authorities.

And what was his sin? Simply translating the 1614 Baptist confession of faith into practical reality. It said, " 'The magistrate is not by virtue of his office to meddle with religion, or matters of conscience, to force or compel men to this or that form of religion, or doctrine; but to leave Christian religion free, to every man's conscience, and to handle only civil transgressions' " (McGlothlin, "Baptist Confession of Faith," p. 82; cited by Longacre, p. 16).

Roger Williams had seen enough of church-state en-

tanglement in England. He had known of the trial of Dr.
Leighton, who had joined the Puritans. Archbishop Laud,
a Protestant himself, had condemned him. Laud's judicial
sentence provided that Dr. Leighton be " 'committed to
the prison of the Fleet for life, and pay a fine of ten
thousand pounds; that the High Commission should de-
grade him from his ministry; and that he should be
brought to the pillory at Westminster while the court was
sitting and be publicly whipped; after whipping be set
upon a pillory [at] a convenient time and have one of his
ears cut off, one side of his nose split, and be branded in
the face with a double S.S. for a sower of sedition; that
then he should be carried back to prison, and after a few
days be pilloried a second time in Cheapside, and have
the other side of his nose split and his other ear cut off,
and then be shut up in close prison for the rest of his life' "
(Longacre, p. 48).

Yes, Roger Williams had seen enough. He would not
tolerate in the New World that from which he had fled in
the Old. He would deny the right of the state to enforce
religion. As a result of his deep convictions, Roger
Williams sparked controversy in Massachusetts. In 1635
the Massachusetts Bay Colony tried him. Before the
court pronounced its sentence of banishment, it asked if
Williams would care to recant. He stoutly refused. " 'I
shall be ready . . . not only to be bound and banished, but
to die also in New England' " (*ibid.,* pp. 57, 58).

In January of 1636 Roger Williams had to flee from
Salem. A violent blizzard tore at his clothing as he
stepped outside his home. Of this episode he later wrote:
" 'I was unmercifully driven from my chamber to a winter's flight, exposed to the miseries, poverties, neces-
sities, wants, debts, hardships of sea and land in a
banished condition. . . . I was sorely tossed for one four-
teen weeks in a bitter winter season, not knowing what

bread and bed did mean' " (*ibid.*, p. 66).

After a grueling test of endurance, during which he ate roots, nuts, and acorns that he found in the deep snows, he reached the wigwams of the Indians along the Narragansett Bay. Chiefs Massasoit and Canonicus took him in, and later Chief Massasoit granted him the land on which the first truly free settlement in modern history was established—Rhode Island.

Although the Sabbatarian Baptists suffered greatly in the Old World and in the New, Roger Williams defended them and gave them asylum in Rhode Island. His enemies sent a report back to England that the Rhode Island colony was not keeping the Sabbath. (They meant Sunday, of course.) Roger Williams replied that there was no scripture "abolishing the seventh day." And he added: "You know yourselves do not keep the Sabbath, that is the seventh day" (*SDA Bible Students' Source Book*, p. 986).

Roger Williams' light of complete freedom flickered but did not die. Thomas Jefferson and James Madison are credited with getting the Bill of Rights voted into the Constitution of the United States, and deservedly so. But Roger Williams' insistence on freedom of religion influenced those who lived in Rhode Island after him. Thus in 1787 Rhode Island refused to send delegates to the Constitutional Convention. It also refused to join the thirteen colonies in adopting the proposed Constitution without the Bill of Rights. Eventually the other colonies threatened to break off commercial relations with Rhode Island. Under this pressure Rhode Island finally ratified the new Constitution in May, 1790. However, it wanted assurance that the Bill of Rights would be added. Although the Bill of Rights was a compromise measure to achieve unity, it was also a victory for the future of the United States.

Something frightening had happened in America—religious persecution. Protestantism had proved itself capable of taking up the sword. Freedom from papal domination had not guaranteed religious freedom. The Bill of Rights was intended to guarantee personal liberty. May it ever succeed in its purpose!

Written in American history for all to see is the sad tale of a people who escaped from Europe to worship freely as they saw fit—only to imitate the Papacy for over one hundred years in persecuting dissenters and "sinners."

Roger Williams' and Rhode Island's early insistence on personal freedom and total religious liberty for everyone gave America those seeds of greatness that would propel it to world preeminence.

Chapter 5

The Dilemma Compounded

The dilemma of Protestantism, as we saw in the previous chapter, is that it came out of Catholicism but brought much of the mother church with it. We have discussed the intolerance that characterized early Protestant history. We also noted that in the New World—a land established by men and women seeking freedom from religious oppression—the *oppressed* became the *oppressors*. This failure of the Protestant movement to make a clean break with Catholicism has had consequences unforeseen by friend or foe.

The Reformation began with the inspiring declaration, "The Bible, and the Bible only, is the rule of faith." This battle cry pledged Protestantism to the complete recovery of apostolic truth. Protestantism could not relent in its pursuit of truth and remain true to God. But it did relent. And so Protestantism has rejected the Sabbath of the Bible and has accepted the "day of the sun."

Sunday-keeping is Protestantism's *dilemma compounded*. With no Scripture to support the practice, the Protestant churches have gone the way of their Catholic mother. They have turned to tradition to support their claims. Some of them have even tried to use Scripture in support of their un-Scriptural day of worship. I refer here to the cry from Protestant pulpits all over the world that the Ten Commandment law has been nailed to the cross.

Now, it must be said that the Reformers did not believe this. They not only preached the validity of the Ten Commandments, but they also proclaimed the right of the state to enforce the first table of the Decalogue. The adoption of the pagan holiday Sunday is clearly a historical error. Yet it is proclaimed the Lord's day without any Scriptural authority. Today's practitioners would bend Scripture to serve their purposes. They seize upon the resurrection of Christ as the Scriptural basis for the observance of Sunday. This argument has become a part of the Protestant tradition. And as with Catholicism, tradition has assumed the force of Scripture. This, too, has contributed to the Protestant dilemma.

Martin Luther revived the doctrine of justification by faith. And this apostolic revelation swept like a breath of fresh air through a works-oriented Christendom. But many, then as now, misunderstood this emphasis. "If, indeed, man is saved by grace through faith, then there are no essential works," some mistakenly concluded. They did not realize that works are the fruitage of the faith by which we live. Obedience is therapeutic. It also strengthens the faith that gives it birth. Salvation by grace through faith does not provide us with an escape from responsibility. The apostles consistently taught obedience to the law of God. They believed that obedience was the fruitage of faith. Works were not a means of being saved, but they were an evidence thereof. Obedience demonstrates the effectiveness of God's grace.

Protestantism's recovery of truth came slowly and painfully. The Baptists suffered greatly because of their stand on baptism by immersion. The Wesley brothers met ridicule because of their strict living habits and teachings. John Wesley was invited to dinner. The table was laden liberally with swine's flesh. Pastor Wesley was asked to say the blessing. "Lord, if Thou canst bless what

Thou hast cursed, then bless this food. Amen," he in-
toned.

Yet gradually and inexplicably the search for truth
ground to a halt. Giant Protestant denominations retired
behind brick walls and stained-glass windows. They became creed-bound, and proud of it. This left large seg-
ments of the Protestant population divided, each holding
a different position on vital doctrines of Scripture. And
such division has puzzled sinners, who expect Christians
to speak with a single voice in matters of doctrine. Had all
movements continued their search for truth, they would
have arrived at a common ground, because God is one and
the faith is one. But doctrinal unity does not exist. We
therefore have a protest movement that no longer pro-
tests the doctrinal excesses and un-Scriptural practices of
the mother church.

Failure to achieve doctrinal unity, however, has not
deterred the search for denominational ecumenicity. The
National Council of Churches and the World Council of
Churches have labored untiringly to achieve denominational oneness. The philosophy is, "Let us deemphasize
those points that divide us and highlight those things on
which we can unite."

At their annual gatherings church dignitaries think
it necessary to make decisions on everything from nuclear deployment to abortion. They lecture governments
and influence politicians. The liberal concept that we
may, through man-made policies, usher in the kingdom
of God forms the mainspring of such activities. Refusal to
unite with these councils is viewed with suspicion.
Nevertheless, observers are allowed to monitor the council proceedings.

Conservative religious leaders are also showing a re-
surgence of interest in the political scene. Voters are
being bombarded by evangelical preachers on radio and

television to vote for specific candidates. Some of these TV personalities hope to dictate national policy by a three million to five million voter-registration effort. Many questions arise, of course. What happens if they achieve such political clout? What spiritual reforms would they then demand? Will the secularization of Sunday become something Protestants decry? And is it possible that the energy crisis and the chaotic social conditions could so undermine the fabric of society that our government would turn to the church for help? And, what kind of help would be forthcoming? Would America, under Protestant influence, resort to legislation for the enforcement of religious decrees?

The issue that just may trigger such action is the one most visibly embarrassing to the Protestant world—the Sabbath issue. In their break with Catholicism the Reformers and their successors stopped short of abandoning the heathenish day of rest and worship.

How could they have missed Genesis 2:2, 3 in their study of Scripture? "And on the seventh day God ended his work which he had made; and he rested on the seventh day from all his work which he had made. And God blessed the seventh day, and sanctified it: because that in it he had rested from all his work which God created and made." And the fourth commandment of the Decalogue is unmistakable in its meaning: "Remember the sabbath day, to keep it holy. Six days shalt thou labour, and do all thy work: but the seventh day is the sabbath of the Lord thy God" (Exodus 20:8-10). A glance at the calendar clearly confirms Saturday as the seventh day. Therefore, Saturday is the Sabbath.

The New Testament is equally clear on this matter. Mark calls Friday "the day before the Sabbath" (Mark 15:42). He further declares that the Sabbath was past when Sunday arrived (see Mark 16:1, 2). These and other passages indicate that Saturday was the New Testament Sabbath. And of this day Christ declared Himself Lord: "The Son of man is Lord also of the sabbath" (Mark 2:28). We conclude, therefore, that the "Lord's day" of Revelation 1:10 is Saturday, the seventh day of the week.

The seventh-day Sabbath signifies God's creative power. "In it thou shalt not do any work, thou, nor thy son, nor thy daughter, thy manservant, nor thy maidservant, nor thy cattle, nor thy stranger that is within thy gates: for in six days the Lord made heaven and earth, the sea, and all that in them is, and rested the seventh day: wherefore the Lord blessed the sabbath day, and hallowed it" (Exodus 20:10, 11).

It also signifies God's sanctifying power: "Moreover also I gave them my sabbaths, to be a sign between me and them, that they might know that I am the Lord that sanctify them." "And hallow my sabbaths; and they shall be a sign between me and you, that ye may know that I am the Lord your God" (Ezekiel 20:12, 20).

It was at Creation the only visible symbol of worship existent. In Eden there were no steeples, pulpits, or cathedrals. Only a temple carved out of time—the Sabbath, the seventh day.

Christ Himself considered it a day of worship. "He came to Nazareth, where he had been brought up: and, as his custom was, he went into the synagogue on the sabbath day, and stood up for to read" (Luke 4:16). His followers also observed the Sabbath. "And they returned, and prepared spices and ointments; and rested the sabbath day *according to the commandment*" (Luke 23:56, emphasis supplied).

That the Reformation failed to recover total truth and stopped short of the Sabbath revelation is, indeed, a mystery. And, may I add, it is today Protestantism's chief embarrassment. To cover its shame it invents all kinds of unlikely stories. "The Sabbath was nailed to the cross," some say. But neither Christ nor the apostles knew anything of this. "We live in the New Testament dispensation," we hear. Yes, but it was built on the only existing Scripture at the time—the Old Testament, which Christ and the apostles preached from. "Christ rose from the dead on Sunday," others proclaim. Indeed He did, but did He authorize the observance of a day in commemoration thereof? The answer is no.

Protestantism's arguments are wearing thin. What will it do when its last argument is exposed? Will Protestants turn to the sword to enforce its wishes? I am afraid so!

Chapter 6

Why an Investigative Judgment?

"My little children, these things write I unto you,
that ye sin not. And if any man sin, we have an advocate with the Father, Jesus Christ the righteous" (1
John 2:1).

It is exceedingly hazardous to go on trial without a
defense attorney. Many a time I have sat in a court-
room and watched judicial procedures. Again and again
I have seen men who might have gone free had they
secured the services of an advocate, but instead they
stood alone at the judgment bar and suffered the full
penalty of the law.

1 John 2:1 says that no man need appear before God
without a lawyer. Furthermore, the Advocate made
available to us is the best in the business. His name is
Jesus Christ.

Let us set the court scene. The prophet Daniel saw
it in vision and describes it for us. "As I looked, thrones
were set in place, and the Ancient of Days took his seat.
His clothing was as white as snow; the hair of his head
was white like wool. His throne was flaming with
fire, and its wheels were all ablaze. A river of fire was
flowing, coming out from before him. Thousands
upon thousands attended him; ten thousand
times ten thousand stood before him. The court was
seated, and the books were opened" (Daniel 7:9, 10,

37

NIV*). Here we see the beginning of the investigative phase of the final judgment. During this phase God will determine human destinies.

"Let us hear the conclusion of the whole matter: Fear God, and keep his commandments: for this is the whole duty of man. For God shall bring every work into judgment, with every secret thing, whether it be good, or whether it be evil" (Ecclesiastes 12:13, 14). "We must all appear before the judgment seat of Christ; that every one may receive the things done in his body, according to that he hath done, whether it be good or bad" (2 Corinthians 5:10).

The solemn work of judgment once begun goes on to completion. It is good to know that we have an intercessor in court, because "he is able also to save them to the uttermost that come unto God by him, seeing he ever liveth to make intercession for them" (Hebrews 7:25). It is good to know that we have a mediator there, "for there is one God, and one mediator between God and men, the man Christ Jesus" (1 Timothy 2:5). It is good to know that we have a substitute there, "now to appear in the presence of God for us" (Hebrews 9:24). The Intercessor, the Mediator, the Substitute, are all one and the same person—Jesus Christ.

But take note that He has also become our judge: "I charge thee therefore before God, and the Lord Jesus Christ, who shall judge the quick [the living] and the dead" (2 Timothy 4:1).

Many people ask, "Why is an investigative judgment necessary? Doesn't God already know everyone who is safe to save?" The Bible supplies a ready answer. In the Garden of Eden, after Adam and Eve sinned, an interest-

---

*From The New International Version. Copyright © 1973, 1978 by The New York Bible Society International and is used by permission.

ing thing happened: "They heard the voice of the Lord God walking in the garden in the cool of the day: and Adam and his wife hid themselves from the presence of the Lord God amongst the trees of the garden. And the Lord God called unto Adam, and said unto him, Where art thou?" (Genesis 3:8, 9).

Let us reconstruct the picture. Adam and Eve had violated God's law. Christ came to conduct a thorough investigation of the case before executing sentence. Verses 10 through 19 give a detailed record of that first investigative judgment. Those who had committed sin were allowed to testify in their own behalf. Only after weighing the testimony did God pronounce sentence upon them. He condemned them to expulsion from the Garden that had been their home since their creation. But He did not execute without first investigating. There is a reason for this. Succeeding generations would read this story, and their judgment of God would, in a sense, hinge on God's treatment of man at the first infraction. The investigation, then, showed us that God is fair and just and, therefore, worthy of our trust and love.

Have you heard of the cities of Sodom and Gomorrah? Homosexuality was so openly practiced in both cities that God could no longer delay judgment. But before judgment was executed (we can read the interesting account in Genesis 18:20, 21), God investigated: "The Lord said, Because the cry of Sodom and Gomorrah is great, and because their sin is very grievous; I will go down now, and see whether they have done altogether according to the cry of it, which is come unto me; and if not, I will know."

Surely God already knew the reputation of Sodom and Gomorrah and all that went on in those wicked cities. He came down not for His sake but for the sake of man. He wanted us who would read of the fiery destruction of Sodom and Gomorrah to know that this was no arbitrary act on His part. He had indeed weighed the evidence. He had patiently endured the insult against His integrity. He had borne long with a people who had become so debased that they were living on the level of animals. Their very presence on the planet was an insult to the Creator. He wanted everyone in succeeding ages to understand that He does not act hastily but gives ample opportunity for repentance. He offers us every marvelous provision of divine grace. But He also wants us all to know that when we reject His grace, we will bear the consequences for our transgressions. Those who reject Christ pay for their own sins.

How long God's solemn work of investigation will continue, no one can say. We know that it began with the righteous. "The time is come that judgment must begin at the house of God: and if it first begin at us, what shall the end be of them that obey not the gospel of God?" (1 Peter 4:17).

We can thank God that the moments of probation still linger. We may still come boldly to the throne of grace and obtain mercy. We can still surrender our lives to Christ. We can still repent of our sins. We can still communicate with Him in prayer and know that He hears us. We can still receive pardon, peace, and power from the only True Source of these graces. And so I appeal to you, dear reader, in the language of Isaiah: "Seek ye the Lord while he may be found, call ye upon him while he is near: let the wicked forsake his way, and the unrighteous man his thoughts: and let him return unto the Lord, and he will have mercy upon him; and to our God, for he will abundantly pardon" (Isaiah 55:6, 7).

Someday we will no longer hear the call of mercy. Christ will have ceased His intercession for man. The unrepentant sinner will have no advocate.

"The day of the Lord will come as a thief in the night;

in the which the heavens shall pass away with a great noise, and the elements shall melt with fervent heat, the earth also and the works that are therein shall be burned up. Seeing then that all these things shall be dissolved, what manner of persons ought ye to be in all holy conversation and godliness, looking for and hasting unto the coming of the day of God, wherein the heavens being on fire shall be dissolved, and the elements shall melt with fervent heat? Nevertheless we, according to his promise, look for new heavens and a new earth, wherein dwelleth righteousness" (2 Peter 3:10-13).

Lawbreakers summoned to court are wise to hire a lawyer. Sinners guilty of breaking God's law should secure the services of Heaven's only recognized Advocate—Jesus Christ. "My little children, . . . if any man sin, we have an advocate with the Father, Jesus Christ the righteous."

Chapter 7

1844

A friend of mine visited his sister and brother-in-law. One night as they played with a Ouija board, they asked my friend to join them. He declined. Then he said, "I'll give you a question for the Ouija. Ask it if there is a Christian in the room."

When they did, the Ouija answered, "Yes," and upon further questioning, it identified my friend as the Christian.

"Ask it one more question," he suggested. "Ask it when the judgment began in heaven."

The Ouija replied, "1-8-4-4."

Despite his questionable approach, the man had wrung from demons a significant admission. Devils are aware of the judgment hour.

"And he said unto me, Unto two thousand and three hundred days; then shall the sanctuary be cleansed" (Daniel 8:14). Daniel had been concerned about the deliverance of Israel. And it is quite possible he interpreted the answer to mean that the captivity of Israel would continue for an extended period, since the prophet fainted.

Ezekiel 4:5, 6 indicates that the prophetic day is a literal year: "For I have laid upon thee the years of their iniquity, according to the number of the days, three hundred and ninety days: so shalt thou bear the iniquity of the house of Israel. And when thou hast accomplished them, lie again on thy right side, and thou shalt bear the iniquity of the house of Judah forty days: I have appointed thee each day for a year." If Daniel understood that one day was equal to one year, then he could have felt very perplexed. Undoubtedly this is why God commissioned the angel Gabriel: "Make this man to understand the vision" (Daniel 8:16). But Gabriel's explanation boggled Daniel's mind, and the prophet fainted. Thus chapter 9 continues Gabriel's explanation: "He informed me, and talked with me, and said, O Daniel, I am now come forth to give thee skill and understanding. At the beginning of thy supplications the commandment came forth, and I am come to shew thee; for thou art greatly beloved: therefore understand the matter, and consider the vision" (Daniel 9:22, 23).

The 2300-year period requires a starting point. The angel supplies it: "Know therefore and understand, that from the going forth of the commandment to restore and to build Jerusalem unto the Messiah the Prince shall be seven weeks, and threescore and two weeks: the street shall be built again, and the wall, even in troublous times" (verse 25). At the time of the prophecy, Israel still languished in captivity, and Jerusalem lay desolate. The Medo-Persian rulers issued three decrees for the return to Jerusalem and the rebuilding of the temple. Ezra 6:14 says, "The elders of the Jews builded, and they prospered through the prophesying of Haggai the prophet and Zechariah the son of Iddo. And they builded, and finished it, according to the commandment of the God of Israel, and according to the commandment of Cyrus, and Darius, and Artaxerxes king of Persia."

Artaxerxes issued the last decree in the seventh year of his reign: "And there went up some of the chil-

dren of Israel, and of the priests, and the Levites, and
the singers, and the porters, and the Nethinims, unto
Jerusalem, in the seventh year of Artaxerxes the king.
And he came to Jerusalem in the fifth month, which
was in the seventh year of the king. For upon the first
day of the first month began he to go up from Babylon,
and on the first day of the fifth month came he to
Jerusalem, according to the good hand of his God upon
him" (Ezra 7:7-9). The seventh year of Artaxerxes was
457 BC. It, then, sets the date for the beginning of the
2300-year prophecy, which contains many interesting
and significant events.

Daniel 9:23, 24 designates the first four hundred
and ninety years of this period as a time of spiritual
privilege for the Jewish nation. It says, "Understand
the matter, and consider the vision. Seventy weeks are
determined upon thy people and upon the holy city, to
finish the transgression, and to make an end of sins,
and to make reconciliation for iniquity, and to bring in
everlasting righteousness, and to seal up the vision and
prophecy, and to anoint the most Holy."

The first sixty-nine weeks of years ($69 \times 7 = 483$ days,
or 483 years) would extend to "Messiah the Prince."
"Know therefore and understand, that from the going
forth of the commandment to restore and to build
Jerusalem unto the Messiah the Prince shall be seven
weeks, and threescore and two weeks: the street shall
be built again, and the wall, even in troublous times"
(Daniel 9:25). Counting from 457 BC, 483 years would
reach to AD 27, the year of Christ's baptism. The word
Messiah means "an anointed one." It was at His baptism that the Holy Spirit visibly anointed Christ. Historically, it was in the fifteenth year of the reign of
Tiberius Caesar that John came preaching and baptiz-
ing.

"Now in the fifteenth year of the reign of Tiberius Caesar, Pontius Pilate being governor of Judaea, and Herod being tetrarch of Galilee, and his brother Philip tetrarch of Ituraea and of the region of Trachonitis, and Lysanias the tetrarch of Abilene, Annas and Caiaphas being the high priests, the word of God came unto John the son of Zacharias in the wilderness. And he came into all the country about Jordan, preaching the baptism of repentance for the remission of sins" (Luke 3:1-3). Notice the scripture states that Pontius Pilate was governor of Judea, which meant it must have been after AD 26 when Pilate became procurator. The rule of Tiberius brings us to AD 27, the year of our Lord's baptism. Thus ended the sixty-nine weeks of years.

Scripture also pictured the crucifixion of Christ: "And he shall confirm the covenant with many for one week: and in the midst of the week he shall cause the sacrifice and the oblation to cease, and for the overspreading of abominations he shall make it desolate, even until the consummation, and that determined shall be poured upon the desolate" (Daniel 9:27). "And after threescore and two weeks shall Messiah be cut off, but not for himself" (verse 26). Three and a half years beyond AD 27 points to AD 31 as the date of the Crucifixion, in the middle of the seventieth week of years. Three and a half years later the mob stoned Stephen, ending the four hundred and ninety years allotted the Jews to "make an end of sins." After AD 34 the apostles turned to the Gentile world with the word that the Jews had taken so lightly. Gentile Christian churches soon dotted the paths of the early church pioneers. Though few realized it, the church had turned a corner and would not look back until the Good News of the kingdom encircled the planet.

Time marched on, and 1,810 years later, the 2300

years expired. At that time the most solemn and momentous period in human history commenced: "the cleansing of the sanctuary." In the Hebrew sanctuary service, this phrase signified the judging of the people. Bishop Fulton Sheen once said, "A tremendous amount of garbage has accumulated in the universe, and must be disposed of." Adventists learned that the record in heaven must be expunged.

Daniel pictured the 1844 judgment scene as follows: "I beheld till the thrones were cast down, and the Ancient of days did sit, whose garment was white as snow, and the hair of his head like the pure wool: his throne was like the fiery flame, and his wheels as burning fire. A fiery stream issued and came forth from before him: thousand thousands ministered unto him, and ten thousand times ten thousand stood before him: the judgment was set, and the books were opened" (Daniel 7:9, 10). These verses picture the beginning of the removal of the record of "accumulated garbage."

Few will deny that there is a temple in heaven. Revelation 11:19 says, "And the temple of God was opened in heaven, and there was seen in his temple the ark of his testament: and there were lightnings, and voices, and thunderings, and an earthquake, and great hail." Then in Revelation 15:5-8: "And after that I looked, and, behold, the temple of the tabernacle of the testimony in heaven was opened: . . . and the temple was filled with smoke from the glory of God, and from his power; and no man was able to enter into the temple, till the seven plagues of the seven angels were fulfilled." It is in this temple that Christ began His "holy place" ministry upon His ascension. It was a work of mediation (1 Timothy 2:5), intercession (Hebrews 7:25), and substitution. In 1844 Christ's ministry in heaven entered the judgment phase.

Ellen White pictures Christ entering the most holy place of the heavenly temple. Intercession, mediation, and substitution still continue, although the judgment has begun. The door of mercy stands ajar, although destinies are being decided. Probation will close for the human family when Christ completes His judgment ministry. "He that is unjust, let him be unjust still: and he which is filthy, let him be filthy still: and he that is righteous, let him be righteous still: and he that is holy, let him be holy still. And, behold, I come quickly; and my reward is with me, to give every man according as his work shall be" (Revelation 22:11, 12).

How sad that a sleeping world races to its date with destiny, not knowing that its case even now stands before the bar of God! The scoffers who laughed at those mistaken believers who expected Christ to return in 1844 will yet be brought to grief over that very date. For while it did not signal the coming to the earth of our Creator and Redeemer, it did, indeed, usher the world into the antitypical day of atonement.

Signs on the earth indicate this: "The nations were angry, and thy wrath is come, and the time of the dead, that they should be judged, and that thou shouldest give reward unto thy servants the prophets, and to the saints, and them that fear thy name, small and great; and shouldest destroy them which destroy the earth" (Revelation 11:18). The glue that holds humanity together is coming unstuck. The very fabric of human society disintegrates. Nature itself reacts to man's retreat from decency, honesty, and righteousness. The serious happenings in heaven produce a serious, nervous reaction on earth. The prophet pictures angels moving in hurried anticipation of something precipitously climactic. Can it be that the judgment of the living is nearing its end? Are we nearer the coming of the Lord than we realize? The attitudes and behavior of the saints should reflect this concern.

Yet, church-leadership circles feel concern that a Laodicean malaise has gripped far too many of the saints. A false sense of security prevails, even though soon the death angel will wing his way to the earth. The blood must be on the doorpost of every heart before the midnight wail of the lost spreads through the land. Where is the judgment-hour intensity that should and must be seen in the church's outreach activity?

As I pen this appeal I am in the midst of an evangelistic effort in Birmingham, Alabama. Tonight I will look into hundreds of expectant, upturned faces that conceal minds hungry for the Bread of life. They are sheep—not now of the Master's fold but thirsting for water from the Master's cistern. Seven nights a week they come, night after passing night. Hunger? Thirst? Desire? It is all there. The harvest is plenteous. The fields are white with waving grain, but the laborers are few.

What will it take to arouse God's people? Must catastrophe tear us from our television screens and dump us into the streets in search of the lost? How long will fear, love of ease, and plain old lack of concern continue to paralyze the spread of God's Good News? When will our love for God overcome these negative characteristics? Heaven is longing for us to shake off our lethargy. Our minds are heavy with knowledge, but we don't always use it wisely. The needs of lost humanity shout at us in every news headline. Sodom and Gomorrah live again before our very eyes. Dare we hesitate another day to communicate truth?

"On the plains of hesitation bleached the bones of countless millions."

Chapter 8

Three Messages to the World!

"Fear God, and give glory to him; for the hour of his judgment is come: and worship him that made heaven, and earth, and the sea, and the fountains of waters" (Revelation 14:7). Although the messenger of Revelation 14:6 flies "in the midst of heaven," his message is for "them that dwell on the earth." Clearly, the messengers are human, for it is through men that the Word of God is carried. From Noah, a preacher of righteousness, to our day, this has been and is the divine plan.

The first message enjoins respect and reverence for and awe of the Almighty. The message calls for us to accept His authority, to revere His person, and to obey His will. It is thus that we fear God and give glory to Him. But the message continues: "Worship him that made heaven, and earth, and the sea, and the fountains of waters." Worship is the most intimate relationship possible between persons. It always involves the lesser and the Greater, the creature and the Creator. That mankind can make soul contact with God is the very heart of worship itself.

Involved also in the call to worship is the day of worship, the holy Sabbath. The very language of the Sabbath commandment, Exodus 20:11, is used in Revelation 14:7. Clearly, Heaven respects the person who acknowledges God as Creator of "heaven and earth, the sea, and all that

in them is." God's designated rest day is an essential
ingredient of that recognition, for the Sabbath is God's
seventh act of Creation. As such, it is as fundamental to
life as are air, water, light, and vegetation. It is not only a
sign of creation but also of God's redemptive act: "Hallow
my sabbaths; and they shall be a sign between me and
you, that ye may know that I am the Lord your God"
(Ezekiel 20:20). Spiritual rest in Christ and rest from
physical labor and secular enterprises are essential to our
well-being. The message of the first angel must be given
worldwide exposure!

Mysteriously, the presentation of the Sabbath at an
evangelistic meeting is decisive in the total decision-
making process. It is the point of no return that affects the
total outlook of the new believer. When understood in its
true light, it is seen to involve the whole man—body,
mind, and spirit. Perhaps it is in this sense that the
Sabbath is *the seal* of God.

The fact that the Sabbath seal involves the name of
the King, His office, and His dominion has deeper impli-
cations than one would at first suspect. Even the commandment to love has the same essentials: "Thou shalt
love the Lord thy God with all thy heart, and with all thy
soul, and with all thy mind" (Matthew 22:37). Love is the
character of God. It therefore contains all of the essential
elements of our King's seal. His name is "the Lord." His
title is "thy God." His territory is the heart, the mind, and
the soul. Only the love of God can prepare the mind for the
will of God. No teaching is theologically sound or spiritually beneficial that does not begin with this. Basic conversion begins here. All else that is meaningful evolves
therefrom. Obedience is valid only as it springs naturally
from a love-filled heart.

The Ten Commandments best express the will of God:
"I delight to do thy will, O my God: yea, thy law is within

my heart" (Psalm 40:8). Internal commitment to God's will must mother external conformity, else the obedient act is the response of a slave—not of a son. With this understanding, we can view the fourth commandment of the law in its awesome spiritual significance. It does contain all the components of the King's seal: "Remember the sabbath day, to keep it holy. Six days shalt thou labour, and do all thy work: but the seventh day is the sabbath of the Lord thy God: in it thou shalt not do any work, thou, nor thy son, nor thy daughter, thy manservant, nor thy maidservant, nor thy cattle, nor thy stranger that is within thy gates: for in six days the Lord made heaven and earth, the sea, and all that in them is, and rested the seventh day: wherefore the Lord blessed the sabbath day, and hallowed it" (Exodus 20:8-11). The true Sabbath observer gives visible evidence of his allegiance to Jehovah. It is unmistakable.

During 1951 in the city of Orlando, Florida, I preached a decision-making sermon that deeply moved the congregation. While shaking hands at the close of the service, a man with a tear-stained face approached me and said, "If I take this step, my employer has stated that he will fire me, and my wife has vowed to leave me. What shall I do?"

Heart wrenching though it was, I could only encourage him to seek the kingdom first. I was sure the "Lord would make a way somehow."

He made his decision for baptism. On the day that it took place, we had special prayer for him while we stood in the baptismal pool.

During the afternoon service, I saw him sitting close to a young lady and holding her hand. At the close of the service I asked him who she was, and he told me, "This is my wife."

"Well, what happened?" I asked, sharing his joy.

He replied, "When I arrived home after my baptism, my wife met me at the door, hugged me, and said, 'Take me out to that tent! If what they are teaching is more important to you than me, then I need it too!' "

She also was baptized—the next Sabbath. But his employer kept his word and fired him. The next three weeks were testing ones. He could not find a hint of employment from any source. Then came the break. A Seventh-day Adventist electrician hired him, and he was on his way. He remains faithful to this day. It was the Sabbath test that brought him to a final decision.

The second angel of Revelation 14 (verse 8) speaks of the fall of the Papacy: "Babylon is fallen, is fallen, that great city, because she made all nations drink of the wine of the wrath of her fornication." The Tower of Babel became the point of confusion when God confounded the languages of man. Subsequently Babylon, with its pagan religious forms, sowed spiritual confusion on an empire-wide scale. But by the time John prophesied, the Babylonian empire was extinct. He was, therefore, referring to an existing order, or one to come. Indeed, it was even then on the way. Catholicism was to unite with civil power to produce a monolithic force that would dominate the world for 1260 years. Religion, science, art, and politics would be subject to the papal power. If this is not the Babylon of Revelation 14, none but the devil himself can qualify, and John treats him as a separate entity.

The Roman Church fell from grace when she dared to tamper with divine law. Daniel the prophet had predicted it: "He shall speak great words against the most High, and shall wear out the saints of the most High, and think to change times and laws: and they shall be given into his hand until a time and times and the dividing of time" (Daniel 7:25). The fulfillment of this prophecy in the experience of the Roman Church is a matter of historical record. The Christian church at Rome stood at the capital of the empire. Persecution by the pagan Roman government was often felt heaviest here because of Christianity's proximity and high visibility in Rome itself. Its leaders feared extinction unless compromise was reached. The church thus began to yield her principles. She adopted the pagan Sunday as a day of worship. She brought in images as objects of veneration. She perverted baptism and substituted penance for repentance. Free grace yielded, in her teachings, to a program of achievement. Eventually such distortions as the selling of indulgences became widespread.

But the sin of Rome does not end here. She employed the arm of civil government to enforce her will on the world. Resistance was condemned as heresy, and the punishment was torture, banishment, or death. Countless martyrs paid with their lives for their allegiance to principle. Bishop Polycarp, of Smyrna, who was burned at the stake, was typical of thousands of others. Politically, the nations vied for Rome's favor. The more harsh their treatment of the innocent, the greater their favor with Rome. They thus became drunk with "the wine . . . of her fornication." "Babylon is fallen, is fallen," the second angel cried.

"And the third angel followed them, saying with a loud voice, If any man worship the beast and his image, and receive his mark in his forehead, or in his hand, the same shall drink of the wine of the wrath of God, which is poured out without mixture into the cup of his indignation; and he shall be tormented with fire and brimstone in the presence of the holy angels, and in the presence of the Lamb" (Revelation 14:9, 10). This messenger perceives the Catholic Church as uniting with the state to form the beast (Papacy) of Revelation 13:1. The image of the beast (apostate Protestantism) is deliberately injected here.

For in the New World she will duplicate the atrocities of
the Middle Ages. It is ironic that Protestantism, which
began with such great promise, will in free America resort to the sword for the enforcement of its will. The mark
of the beast (Sunday worship) would be adopted by a
church (Protestantism) that was raised up by God to
pursue truth to its ultimate revelation. But Protestants
clung to the papal day and brought it to the New World.
And, as we learned in an earlier chapter, Protestantism
enforced Sunday-keeping by law. John gives us in this
chapter the unwelcome news that Protestantism will imitate Catholicism and turn the New World into a caldron
of confusion. The specter of persecution here seems impossible now. But prophecy cannot fail. The flood tide of
bloodletting will reach these shores. It is the dictate of
God.

The world must have a clear choice. The claims of
God's law must be clearly understood before the beast's
mark can be applied. This does not lessen the claim of
God's holy Sabbath here and now. People who understand
truth but refuse to obey it suffer the same fate as those
who later receive the mark of the beast. The significance
of the mark is that it identifies the transgressor to the
destroying angel when the plagues fall. Just as in ancient
Egypt the blood provided to the angel of death a guide not
to kill, so in this last test the mark of the beast (Sunday
worship) will provide a sure guide to the angel as to who
should fall.

Is not this the day of grace—to make doubly sure that
we have the seal of God? The perils of the last days are
upon us. Today there is no hand to stay the approaching
doom. As with ancient Sodom, the planet is too far gone to
reclaim. Sinful man seems hypnotized in his measured
march to perdition. Calamities seem only to make him
blaspheme. The gospel of Christ, while rescuing some, is

viewed with contempt by the great majority. The grapes of wrath, though stored (but not for long), will feel the tread of the King of kings. Their bloodred juices, symbolic of the wicked dead, will rise to the horses' bridles.

Chapter 9

The Remnant Church

Significantly, the hour of God's judgment in heaven signaled the small beginnings of what has become a world movement. The preaching of William Miller had encouraged thousands to expect the coming of Christ to the earth in 1844. When Christ did not come, those earnest Christians suffered deep and bitter disappointment. Their experience of disillusionment resembled that of the disciples at the Crucifixion. Jesus' first disciples fully expected Him to establish an earthly kingdom as a result of His first coming.

Some Christians today feel that Judas betrayed Him to hasten the process. Judas never dreamed that Christ would submit to the indignities that followed His arrest. In his frustration at what he saw, Judas flung the "blood money" at the feet of the priests and went out and hanged himself. The other disciples—in embarrassment and fear—hid behind shut doors. They considered Christ's mission and their own a failure. Their gloom was not lifted until Mary brought them the good news of the empty tomb. This experience and subsequent revelations sent them on their way rejoicing as they preached the gospel of the kingdom.

The recovery of the faithful Adventists in 1844 was no less spectacular. Hiram Edson's report of his new insight sent the pioneers to the Bible, where they found good news that sent them on their way. God had come suddenly to the holy of holies, and the message of the judgment must go to the nations before Christ would come to the earth.

Only a remnant of the Millerite believers, however, held together and clung to their faith. Among them was James White. He deserves mention here for the pivotal role he played in the growth and polity of the Seventh-day Adventist Church. His public evangelism was a model for succeeding generations. Despite many dangers, he boldly braved angry mobs to proclaim the faith. Hundreds flocked to the Advent banner. His ability as an organizer laid the foundation for the organizational structure of the Seventh-day Adventist Church, which now circles the globe.

That there is an invisible remnant the Scriptures plainly teach. "And other sheep I have, which are not of this fold: them also I must bring, and they shall hear my voice; and there shall be one fold, and one shepherd" (John 10:16). Scattered throughout Christendom are sincere followers of Christ whom our Lord calls His own. Imprisoned by tradition, creeds, and social ties, many of them know nothing of God's special message for these times. To them we must carry the word with all urgency! Sands in the hourglass of time run low as the "times of the Gentiles" run their course. Humanity threatens itself with nuclear suicide. Thousands look wistfully toward heaven, thirsting for God's last word for the last generation. The visible remnant must move to meet this need!

Scripture clearly identifies the visible remnant. "And the dragon was wroth with the woman, and went to make war with the remnant of her seed, which keep the commandments of God, and have the testimony of Jesus Christ" (Revelation 12:17). "Here is the patience of the saints: here are they that keep the commandments of

God, and the faith of Jesus" (Revelation 14:12). The
church of the Second Coming must clearly reflect this
twofold emphasis. It must declare unequivocally that
Christ alone is Saviour and that the jurisdiction of His
law is universal and perpetual. Let us examine these
principles in some depth.

"The testimony of Jesus" is both *about Him and of
Him*. "The faith of Jesus" is both *of Him and about Him*.
Jesus Himself first expounded these principles that concern Him and His saving grace toward men. When the
angels sang at His earthly birth, "Glory to God in the
highest, and on earth peace, good will toward men" (Luke
2:14), their message was, indeed, "glad tidings of great
joy" to the earth. And what is this Good News? "For unto
you is born this day in the city of David a Saviour, which
is Christ the Lord" (Luke 2:11). Note that He is born
"unto you"—to each of us. He is personal Lord and
Saviour to the believer. Salvation centers in Him and in
His demonstration in behalf of man. And that demonstration is fivefold: (1) His incarnation, (2) His crucifixion,
(3) His resurrection, (4) His priestly ministry, and
(5) His second coming.

The Incarnation is of supreme importance to man, for
in a real sense Christ identifies with the human family:
"And the Word was made flesh, and dwelt among us, (and
we beheld his glory, the glory as of the only begotten of
the Father,) full of grace and truth" (John 1:14). God took
on the problems of man *as a man*. He is, to be sure, the
God-man, but He fought no battle with sin or Satan as
God. He voluntarily tabled His divinity in the struggle
with sin, and He overcame for thirty-three years, never
losing a single battle. It is remarkable that He would take
on the legions of hell, but by depending on the Holy
Ghost, He won. Yet He accepted all the risks involved so
that He might bring us to God. And there were risks.

Eternal separation from His Father would have been His fate had He yielded to evil for just one moment. But through prayer, fasting, and helping others, He fought His way to the cross. His epic struggle has deep significance for all humanity. It offers us an absolute perfection that we cannot otherwise obtain. More about this in the next chapter.

In a real sense Christ became one of us that we might become one with Him. He was born in a manger. No one could come here under worse conditions. The lowest outcast is upstaged by His circumstances of birth. Furthermore, to the casual observer Jesus was born under suspicious circumstances, which His enemies later taunted Him over. "We be not born of fornication," they said in John 8:41. How could they have known in their blindness that God was His Father and that by a process known to God alone, Mary had conceived Him of the Holy Ghost? How could they have known that in dealing with Christ they were in contact with a heavenly royalty? The Negro spiritual is right: "Poor little Jesus Boy; They made you be born in a manger. Poor little Holy Child, didn't know who You were." But His ministry to mankind was just beginning. He came to live for us, and live He did! But He also came to die.

The Crucifixion climaxed Christ's earthly struggle with Satan. Since childhood Christ had managed to frustrate Satan at every turn. After face-to-face combat in the wilderness, Satan stumbled stricken from the desert sands in defeat. But he came back again and again, and with the same results. Now, at Golgotha—with the Son of God pinned to a tree—he had only hours to accomplish what he had failed to do in years. Satan unleashed the full fury of hell at Calvary but to no avail.

Christ was at His majestic best on the hill that day. No one ever died like He did. In His innocence, pressured toward the grave by the sins of the world, He was the essence of selflessness. And as such, He was a source of frustration for Lucifer and his hordes. All hell was on the hill that day. And the cup of man's salvation trembled in Christ's nail-pierced hands. He drained its very dregs before He died. "He was wounded for our transgressions, he was bruised for our iniquities: the chastisement of our peace was upon him; and with his stripes we are healed. All we like sheep have gone astray; we have turned every one to his own way; and the Lord hath laid on him the iniquity of us all" (Isaiah 53:5, 6). Jesus tasted hell for us so that we might enjoy heaven. He has remitted our sins and opened a door of hope for all mankind.

The Resurrection is described in the following language: "And, behold, there was a great earthquake: for the angel of the Lord descended from heaven, and came and rolled back the stone from the door, and sat upon it." "And the angel answered and said unto the women, Fear not ye: for I know that ye seek Jesus, which was crucified. He is not here: for he is risen, as he said. Come, see the place where the Lord lay" (Matthew 28:2, 5, 6).

The apostle Paul is very painstaking in his supportive evidence of the Resurrection. He says, "I delivered unto you first of all that which I also received, how that Christ died for our sins according to the scriptures; and that he was buried, and that he rose again the third day according to the scriptures: and that he was seen of Cephas, then of the twelve: after that, he was seen of above five hundred brethren at once; of whom the greater part remain unto this present, but some are fallen asleep. After that, he was seen of James; then of all the apostles. And last of all he was seen of me also, as of one born out of due time" (1 Corinthians 15:3-8).

The resurrection of Christ places Him above and beyond the founders of all rival religions. He alone rose from the dead. That He is alive validates His divinity and mission. "Now if Christ be preached that he rose from the dead, how say some among you that there is no resurrection of the dead? But if there be no resurrection of the dead, then is Christ not risen: and if Christ be not risen, then is our preaching vain, and your faith is also vain. Yea, and we are found false witnesses of God; because we have testified of God that he raised up Christ: whom he raised not up, if so be that the dead rise not. For if the dead rise not, then is not Christ raised: and if Christ be not raised, your faith is vain; ye are yet in your sins. Then they also which are fallen asleep in Christ are perished" (verses 12-18). And further, He guaranteed our own resurrection.

Christ ascended on high to perform the significant services described in an earlier chapter. As our High Priest, He does for us what no one else could do. He had earlier told the disciples, "Nevertheless I tell you the truth; It is expedient for you that I go away: for if I go not away, the Comforter will not come unto you; but if I depart, I will send him unto you" (John 16:7). What Christ was to do in heaven, He alone could do. He would be our Intercessor, Mediator, Substitute, and Judge. The Holy Spirit took up the work of Christ on the earth on a broader scale. Of Christ's ministry in heaven, Paul exults, "For such an high priest became us, who is holy, harmless, undefiled, separate from sinners, and made higher than the heavens" (Hebrews 7:26).

His second coming will serve as a fitting climax to the "testimony of Jesus" aspect of the message of the remnant. We must especially stress the nearness of that coming. Prophetic writings must be brought to bear on this subject. We must closely monitor world events in this connection. God has not told us the day or the hour, but we may know the "times and seasons."

Scripture clearly reveals the cataclysmic events connected with our Lord's return. The death of the wicked, the resurrection of the righteous, the glorification of the saints, and the devastation of the earth all form part of this. The millennium, the resurrection of the wicked, hellfire, and the re-creation and revitalization of this planet will follow in their order. Thus Christ's efforts in our behalf will be completed, and humanity will have its jubilee!

A benign form of grace has made insidious progress in our world, but it is a grace that denies the jurisdiction of law. The remnant church now has its work cut out for it. It must assert the efficacy of grace while it also proclaims the perpetuity of law. Repentance, faith, and conversion lead to basic behavioral change. Men are being judged by the law. "So speak ye, and so do, as they that shall be judged by the law of liberty" (James 2:12). The government of God and His jurisdiction is involved. If God is Lord at all, then He is Lord of all. And His law is no less universal than His grace. The law serves as an educational instrument. "What shall we say then? Is the law sin? God forbid. Nay, I had not known sin, but by the law: for I had not known lust, except the law had said, Thou shalt not covet" (Romans 7:7). The meaning of this to the believer is treated in greater detail in the chapter to follow.

Chapter 10

1888

God's message to the remnant in 1888 focused on salvation by grace through faith. Most of the early Adventists had come from denominations with creeds that even to this day embody this emphasis. The remnant, then, generally agreed on this point, though when cast adrift from the traditional church bodies and forced to articulate these principles, they officially wrote very little on the subject until the church was organized. The book *Steps to Christ* offered much help in this area.

We should also remember that independent Bible study, a cornerstone of the Reformation, has always been an Adventist passion. Scripturally sound conclusions that are independently arrived at are by no means discouraged. We should understand, therefore, that concurrence on points of doctrine was possible only when these issues were hammered out in the crucible of debate. The writer, therefore, is neither disturbed, surprised, nor dismayed at the disagreements and passion that accompanied and followed the 1888 discussions. We are free individuals. Free men differ freely. Unanimity is painfully achieved in this atmosphere. The clash of ideas in prayerful Bible study and constructive debate indicates good health. Coming out of Catholicism, where the fiat of popes often made dissent hazardous, Protestant debate ranged far afield as honest men, guided by the Spirit of

God, groped for the light. But the seeker for truth will not be disappointed, and the year 1888 thus looms large in the history of Adventist doctrinal involvement.

Historically the Advent believers were faced with a crisis of continued belief in the doctrine of the second coming of Christ. They had, after all, set two dates for this grand event, and both had passed uneventfully. The knowledge that Christ in 1844 came "suddenly . . . to his temple" in heaven climaxed continued Bible study and prayer. The doctrine of the Second Coming would henceforth be preached unfettered by time-setting, placing it on a solid Scriptural basis.

The pioneer Adventists were also products of a Protestantism that laid heavy emphasis on grace, but that same Protestantism said precious little about man's obligation to the great laws of God. With their growing knowledge of the origin, scope, and perpetuity of divine law, the voice of the Adventist expositor was and is heard defending those oracles. The Sabbath of the Lord became one of the great "testing" truths for the seeker who is breaking through to the light. The messenger to the remnant sent up a danger signal. Ellen G. White wrote, "We have preached the law until we are as dry as the hills of Gilboa that had neither dew nor rain. We must preach Christ in the law" (*Review and Herald*, March 11, 1890, p. 146). Thus the stage was set for the historic presentations. What the two principal teachers said to the church at that time is of eternal value to the remnant. And what essentially is that message?

"For by grace are ye saved through faith; and that not of yourselves: it is the gift of God" (Ephesians 2:8). Man may not by deeds of righteousness secure his salvation. Salvation is the plan and act of One *external* to the saved. "That at that time ye were without Christ, being aliens from the commonwealth of Israel, and strangers from the covenants of promise, having no hope, and without God in the world: but now in Christ Jesus ye who sometimes were far off are made nigh by the blood of Christ" (verses 12, 13). It is clearly His act that secures our salvation. "Not by works of righteousness which we have done, but according to his mercy he saved us, by the washing of regeneration, and renewing of the Holy Ghost; which he shed on us abundantly through Jesus Christ our Saviour; that being justified by his grace, we should be made heirs according to the hope of eternal life" (Titus 3:5-7).

We should note that the salvation so freely offered is by grace through faith. Furthermore, God gives us the faith by which we claim it. "For I say, through the grace given unto me, to every man that is among you, not to think of himself more highly than he ought to think; but to think soberly, according as God hath dealt to every man the measure of faith" (Romans 12:3). Ellen White has said, "Genuine faith is life" (*The Desire of Ages,* p. 347). Christ has, therefore, given every man the power to contact Him. By faith, sinners become saints, and everyone has a "measure of faith." Each of us has this God-given capacity to reach out to God. Faith is the sixth sense, the power to contact the supernatural. What sight, smell, touch, taste, and hearing cannot do, faith can!

While it is true that God plants within every person the seedling of faith, it is our responsibility to cultivate it and augment its growth. This is possible in three ways: (1) "So then faith cometh by hearing, and hearing by the word of God" (Romans 10:17). The study of God's Word builds faith. To the prayerful student of Scripture, "faith cometh." The Word of God is to the barren soul what air, sunshine, rain, and fertilizer are to the soil. (2) Faith is cultivated by prayer. "Ask, and it shall be given you; seek, and ye shall find; knock, and it shall be opened unto you" (Matthew 7:7). "Increase our faith," was the prayer of the apostles (Luke 17:5). A Father-God, who is more

willing to give gifts to His children than natural parents
are, stands ready to give faith to the earnest seeker.
(3) Exercise is essential to a growing faith. In a sense, all
development involves exercise. Ultimately things boil
down to performance, demonstration, and a visible mani-
festation. A faithful exercise of faith strengthens the
same, and it gives credence, validity, and certification
thereto. The song says correctly: "Each vict'ry will help
you some other to win." Rewarded faith makes a Christian more confident.

The patriarch Job illustrates this. Shorn of his
wealth, his health, his wife's love, and his children, Job
had no visible evidence of God's love. His well-meaning
friends taunted him in his distress. Yet his faith in God
kept him alive. "For I know that my redeemer liveth, and
that he shall stand at the latter day upon the earth: and
though after my skin worms destroy this body, yet in my
flesh shall I see God: whom I shall see for myself, and
mine eyes shall behold, and not another; though my reins
be consumed within me" (Job 19:25-27). Job's ringing
affirmation, "Though he slay me, yet will I trust in him"
(Job 13:15) has become his most famous expression.

Job was irrevocably committed. Not even death or its
prospect could shake his faith in God. He would die *in* the
faith. He would die *for* the faith. His personal faith in the
Source of all faith was impregnable. God's faith in Job
was justified. Satan stood discredited. And Job emerged
from the experience seven times better off for having had
it. His faith in God was vindicated. Centuries later he has
become a prime example of God's goodness and the re-
wards of faith.

"Therefore being justified by faith, we have peace
with God through our Lord Jesus Christ" (Romans 5:1).
God renders man innocent and declares him just on the
basis of saving faith. Christ has by the shedding of blood

secured our pardon. To believe this is to receive the blessing. The Good News of the gospel is that the righteousness of Christ is conferred upon us on the merits of the
Son of God. Because of his acceptance of Christ and apart
from works, the thief on the cross was saved. Though on
the cross, he typified how all men are saved, namely, by
grace through faith. "It is the gift of God: not of works, lest
any man should boast" (Ephesians 2:8, 9). The Good News
is that through saving faith we are justified *before* we are
qualified, accepted *before* we are acceptable, received *before* we have achieved, trusted *before* we are trustworthy.
All of this we experience on the merits of the Son of God
and through our faith in Him.

And this relationship ultimately refines human behavior. Behavioral change is a consequence of the new
relationship. Good deeds do little to appease the Almighty. We can approach Him only through the name of
and the merits of His Son. It is, therefore, clear that faith
in Him, love of Him, and respect for Him are offerings
that move the great heart of God toward man. Let us
examine them separately.

Saving faith is threefold in nature. We must believe
on Him. We must believe *in* Him. And we must *believe*
Him.

To believe *on* Jesus means that we accept His creden-
tials. We believe that He is who He says He is. We accept
the fact of His divinity. This is crucial. "Believe on the
Lord Jesus Christ, and thou shalt be saved" (Acts 16:31).
"Therefore let all the house of Israel know assuredly, that
God hath made that same Jesus, whom ye have crucified,
both Lord and Christ" (Acts 2:36), Peter proclaimed at
Pentecost. Of Himself, Jesus said, "I am Alpha and
Omega, the beginning and the ending, saith the Lord,
which is, and which was, and which is to come, the Al-
mighty" (Revelation 1:8). In Isaiah 9:6 the prophet called

Him "The mighty God." In John 20:28 Thomas acknowl-
edged Him as "my Lord and my God." And Peter insists,
"Neither is there salvation in any other: for there is none
other name under heaven given among men, whereby we
must be saved" (Acts 4:12). The first acknowledgment of
faith, then, is that Jesus Christ is God. "But without faith
it is impossible to please him: for he that cometh to God
must believe that he is, and that he is a rewarder of them
that diligently seek him" (Hebrews 11:6).

It is natural to take the second step of faith after
having made the first. We believe *in* Him. We come to
believe that He can do what He says He can do. Christ has
power unlimited. He is of infinite capacity. No problem
taxes His intellect. No difficulty can resist His solution. It
is this very fact that makes worry a sin, for worry says to
God, "My problem is beyond solution, too great for You,
God." This, of course, insults God. "I know that thou canst
do every thing, and that no thought can be withholden
from thee" (Job 42:2), Job exulted. "But our God is in the
heavens: he hath done whatsoever he hath pleased"
(Psalm 115:3). "Whatsoever the Lord pleased, that did he
in heaven, and in earth, in the seas, and all deep places"
(Psalm 135:6).

He can do what He says He can do. He is able to pardon
iniquity. "Let the wicked . . . return unto the Lord, and he
will have mercy upon him; and to our God, for he will
abundantly pardon" (Isaiah 55:7). He is able to break the
chain of the most powerful, soul-destroying habit. He has
dried out alcoholics, converted prostitutes, and cured
drug addicts. He has given sight to the blind, healed the
lame, and raised the dead. He has given hope to the
hopeless, calmed angry seas, unstopped deaf ears, and
restored broken homes. Our God's saving power defies
contradiction.

To believe in and on Him is essential, but yet another

step is necessary. We must *believe* Him. We must take His word, even though we may find no visible evidence to support it. Beyond this, we must trust Him in the face of seemingly contrary evidence. This third dimension is probably the most difficult. To believe in the face of the storm, when no shaft of light pierces the gloom, is to exercise supreme trust. This is faith at its best—the ultimate dimension. To believe that God can and will help me is laudable. But to believe that God is delivering me now—-in the absence of evidence or in the face of contrary evidence—is the supreme experience of faith. And it is this kind of faith that makes man whole! Our next chapter will deal with the involvements of love, faith, and respect.

Chapter 11

Sinai

God set a mountain on fire when with the following introduction He proclaimed, "I am the Lord thy God, which have brought thee out of the land of Egypt, out of the house of bondage" (Exodus 20:2). It remained for the apostle Paul to identify the member of the Godhead who spoke those words: "And did all drink the same spiritual drink: for they drank of that spiritual Rock that followed them: and that Rock was Christ" (1 Corinthians 10:4). Verse 9 of that same chapter adds, "Neither let us tempt Christ, as some of them also tempted, and were destroyed of serpents." So, it was Christ who thundered the Ten Immortal Words from the smoking mount. When we use the word *law* for the Ten Commandments, we verbally point to the character of God, for God's moral law is His will committed to the language of man. It constitutes the foundation of justice for the universe.

"Wherefore the law was our schoolmaster to bring us unto Christ, that we might be justified by faith. But after that faith is come, we are no longer under a schoolmaster" (Galatians 3:24, 25). The moral law, spanning the centuries between the sin of Adam and the first coming of Christ, served as man's principal instructor. From direct revelation and from the law, prophets and preachers took their themes as they guided men through the maze of error that cluttered the shifting scenes of time.

Christ, the original principal-teacher in the Garden of Eden, communed with man face-to-face. But sin marred all of this. It deprived man of the privilege of face-to-face communion with his Maker. So the law and the prophets as substitute teachers spanned the centuries until John announced Jesus. "The law and the prophets were until John: since that time the kingdom of God is preached, and every man presseth into it" (Luke 16:16). Verse 17 makes it clear that Christ's coming did not abrogate the law: "It is easier for heaven and earth to pass, than one tittle of the law to fail."

With the coming of the Lawgiver Himself, the law was relegated to textbook status. It served as the basis of instruction. For example, Jesus taught, "Ye have heard that it was said by them of old time, Thou shalt not commit adultery: but I say unto you, That whosoever looketh on a woman to lust after her hath committed adultery with her already in his heart" (Matthew 5:27, 28). Christ's teachings cleared the law of all of the multitudinous strictures that tradition-oriented teachers had added to it. In the language of Isaiah, He magnified the law and made it honorable (Isaiah 42:21). Whereas the law and the prophets had served as substitute instructors from the sin of Adam to John, Christ the Master Teacher now came on the scene. He resumed His in-person role as Chief Instructor, and the law, the prophets, and the preachers assumed subordinate roles.

We can compare the relationship of the law to Christ with the role of the moon and stars during the noonday glory of the sun. They still exist and perform their functions even though the sun outshines them and obliterates them from our sight. Similarly, we

must never in our thinking allow the law to compete
with the Lawgiver. We must not regard obedience as
the object of the faith-love relationship. Our love relationship with Christ is an end within itself. We do not
relate to Christ "in order that" anything! Christ is the
end (purpose) of the law. The law is not the end (purpose) of Christ. We do not accept Christ *so that* we may
obey the law. In accepting Christ we are fulfilled.
Obedience is a *natural* consequence of our love—not its
objective. Behavioral change is the symptom of conversion, but it is not the reason for conversion.

There is also a subjective sense in which the law
brings "us unto Christ." Paul spoke from deep personal
conviction in Romans 7:7: "What shall we say then? Is
the law sin? God forbid. Nay, I had not known sin, but
by the law: for I had not known lust, except the law had
said, Thou shalt not covet." Though the major teacher
function was transferred to the Holy Spirit at Christ's
ascension, the law retains an eternal position in the
heavenly university as the chief textbook.

God designed it to show all men their need of a
Saviour. "For if any be a hearer of the word, and not a
doer, he is like unto a man beholding his natural face
in a glass: for he beholdeth himself, and goeth his way,
and straightway forgetteth what manner of man he
was. But whoso looketh into the perfect law of liberty,
and continueth therein, he being not a forgetful hearer,
but a doer of the work, this man shall be blessed in his
deed" (James 1:23-25).

Throughout His lifetime Christ obeyed God's law.
And God places Christ's record and experience of perfect obedience to our account when by faith we accept
Jesus into our lives as Lord and Saviour. The involvements of this contract are complex, but we must understand them. To accept salvation is to commit ourselves

to the ideal of behavioral perfection—while acknowledging the impossibility of the flesh to achieve it. No one, before or since Christ, ever achieved perfection. No one ever will. We can know this fact, and we can accept it, yet at the same time we can aspire to perfection as though it can be reached. Hoping against hope, believing against belief, resisting "unto blood"—this is the "good fight of faith." We fight not to be saved but because we are saved.

At no point in our lives do we see absolute perfection in ourselves. If we think we do, we have deceived ourselves. "If we say that we have no sin, we deceive ourselves, and the truth is not in us. If we confess our sins, he is faithful and just to forgive us our sins, and to cleanse us from all unrighteousness. If we say that we have not sinned, we make him a liar, and his word is not in us" (1 John 1:8-10). Faith is, after all, "the substance of things hoped for, the evidence of things not seen" (Hebrews 11:1).

Though we do not always see behavioral perfection, our faith that perfection will be seen is both the *evidence* and the *means* that better days are on the way! And so Scripture encourages us to live on, fight on, and strive for the mastery. The people listed in Hebrews 11 were just such individuals. Their supreme virtue was their undying faith that the impossible was and is possible. They, therefore, spent their lives "reaching the unreachable star" and fighting past failure to "beat the unbeatable foe."

Chapter 4 of Romans offers us further encouragement. The God of heaven had promised Abraham and Sarah that they would have a baby. Now, Sarah was barren, and Abraham was over one hundred years old. Paul's description of Abraham's body "now dead" and "the deadness of Sarah's womb" reminds us of our own "deadness" in trespasses and sin. But Abraham "staggered not at the promise of God through unbelief; but was strong in faith, giving glory to God; and being fully persuaded that, what he had promised, he was able also to perform. And therefore it was imputed to him for righteousness. Now it was not written for his sake alone, that it was imputed to him; but for us also, to whom it shall be imputed, if we believe on him that raised up Jesus our Lord from the dead; who was delivered for our offences, and was raised again for our justification" (Romans 4:20-24).

Certain facts in Abraham's experience stand out and shout for our attention.

1. Abraham believed God, and he was considered a father nine months before the birth of the baby. God was thus calling "those things which be not as though they were" (verse 17). With His foreknowledge God can do this. The faith of Abraham made the future fulfillment of God's promises a present reality.

It is somewhat like the barefoot slave who looked forward to deliverance by singing, "I got shoes!" Faith brings much of the future glory into the *here and now!*

A little boy, walking around the house empty-handed, kept repeating, "I have an orange."

His mother tried to silence him but in vain. She finally confronted him. "How can you say you have an orange when your hand is empty?"

The little boy replied, "Does Jesus own all of the oranges?"

"Why, yes," answered his mother.

"Well, Jesus has the orange, and I've got Jesus."

2. Abraham's faith resulted in activity that led to the birth of a son. But then, Abraham habitually lived like this. "Abraham obeyed my voice, and kept my charge, my commandments, my statutes, and my

laws" (Genesis 26:5).

Later Abraham passed the supreme test when God ordered him to kill Isaac, the prize he so dearly loved and the child of his faith. Faith is beyond human reason, and those who demand a reasonable faith must come to grips with this fact. In childlike trust, though deeply troubled, Abraham came to grips with his weakness. He had stumbled previously in dealing with Abimelech. He must now demonstrate an unfaltering trust. His faith had grown. He overcame! And an angel stopped the descending dagger.

3. We are saved while we are being saved. Be patient with yourself. Character does not suddenly develop. Like Baby Isaac, our characters come to maturity "in time" as we apply ourselves to the laws of growth—prayer, Bible study, and Christian service. Christian growth involves trial and error. Both are courses in the school of experience. We should closely monitor our attitudes when things go wrong. They will tell us, as nothing else can, if we are saved or lost. Does all that is within you rise up in revulsion at the sinful deed? Do you grimly determine not to repeat the sinful act? Do you feel ashamed that you have betrayed yourself and your Lord? Do you have a deep resolve to atone?

During their moments of remorse the saved recall the words: "When I sit in darkness, the Lord shall be a light unto me" (Micah 7:8) and, "Weeping may endure for a night, but joy cometh in the morning" (Psalm 30:5).

The moral law is perpetual. Psalm 111:7, 8 says, "The works of his hands are verity and judgment; all his commandments are sure. They stand fast for ever and ever, and are done in truth and uprightness." God's law is binding on all men. "Fear God, and keep his commandments: for this is the whole duty of man" (Ecclesiastes 12:13). The law describes the Christian's life-style. It has condemned human nature since Adam's fall. It does not approve of it now. Our very best obedience falls short of the spirit and letter of the law. We, therefore, can never appeal to our deeds for God's approval. Only the covering blood of Christ can secure our acceptance. His life must cover ours even in sanctification. "It is Christ—first, last, and always." If, then, our strictest performance is faulty and unacceptable on its own merits, why perform? Why obey? Why try?

I answer: Will our *faith* in God, our *love* for God, and our *respect* of God allow us to do any less? Of course not. Those are the most powerful motivating forces in the universe. Indeed, the *depth* of our love, the *quality* of our faith, and the *height* of our respect determine the *nature* and *pace* of behavioral change. These Christian virtues impel us to perform beyond the letter of the law. They penetrate to the realm of the attitude so that our desires are disciplined to the spirit of the law, so that as prayerful Christians we don't even want to transgress. In the conflict with human nature, God's will triumphs over the flesh. We become man at his best. And a frustrated Lucifer acknowledges the heavenly hedge about us.

Joseph's performance demonstrates this. Tempted by Potiphar's wife to violate the seventh commandment, he resisted her wiles and the appetites of his own flesh with these immortal words: "How then can I do this great wickedness, and sin against God?" (Genesis 39:9). Joseph made God's will supreme in his life because the relationship was personal. Joseph believed, loved, and respected God. And so he ran for his life. He understood that while keeping the law does not save, breaking it destroys our connection with God. Sin continually committed systematically drives God out of the life. There occurs in consequence a hardening of the conscience and a paralysis of the will. And such an enfeebled person has joined the legions of the damned.

"Seek ye the Lord while he may be found, call ye upon him while he is near: let the wicked forsake his way, and the unrighteous man his thoughts: and let him return unto the Lord, and he will have mercy upon him; and to our God, for he will abundantly pardon" (Isaiah 55:6, 7).

Chapter 12

The Beast and the Buffalo!

Revelation 13 introduces two kingdoms that are uniquely alike and yet widely divergent. Prophecy portrays them as the beast and the "buffalo." Their appearance indicates their dissimilarity. Unfortunately their similarity lies in what the beast set out to do and what the buffalo, in extreme crisis, will ultimately do. A study of both will enlighten the reader as to the past and prepare him for the shocking and momentous future.

The Beast

"And I stood upon the sand of the sea, and saw a beast rise up out of the sea, having seven heads and ten horns, and upon his horns ten crowns, and upon his heads the name of blasphemy. And the beast which I saw was like unto a leopard, and his feet were as the feet of a bear, and his mouth as the mouth of a lion: and the dragon gave him his power, and his seat, and great authority" (Revelation 13:1, 2). In Bible prophecy a beast represents a kingdom, as specified in Daniel: "These great beasts, which are four, are four kings, which shall arise out of the earth" (7:17).

The ten horns on the head of this beast identify it as the successor of the pagan Roman Empire. The ten toes of the image of Daniel 2 also indicate such a division. History confirms this breakup of the empire. Barbarian hordes erased the final vestige of imperial authority. Alaric, Attilla, Odoacer, and others contributed to the dismemberment of the Roman Empire. For over six hundred years decisions made in Rome had made Europe tremble. But political confusion reigned in the wake of Rome's fall in AD 476. From the ruins of this once great empire rose the beast of Revelation 13. "Long ages ago, when Rome was left to the mercy of barbarous hordes, the Romans turned to one figure for aid and protection, and asked him to rule them; and thus, in this simple manner . . . commenced the temporal sovereignty of the Popes" (*American Catholic Quarterly Review,* April, 1911).

John identified the beast by a number. "Here is wisdom. Let him that hath understanding count the number of the beast: for it is the number of a man; and his number is Six hundred threescore and six" (Revelation 13:18). The Papacy for centuries used the forged Donation of Constantine to support its claims that the pope is the vicar of Christ. The Latin title VICARIUS FILII DEI officially designates the popes. The numerical value of this title is as follows:

V	-	5	F	-	0	D	- 500
I	-	1	I	-	1	E	- 0
C	-	100	L	-	50	I	- 1
A	-	0	I	-	1		
R	-	0	I	-	1		
I	-	1					
U	-	5					
S	-	0				TOTAL	- 666

Inspiration has pointed to the Roman Catholic Church and its union with secular political powers as the beast of Revelation 13:1. This union, which dominated Europe during the Middle Ages, is called the Papacy.

Science, art, politics, and religion suffered at the hands of papal decrees and edicts for 1260 years—from AD 538 to AD 1798. The church's ability to use the sword of temporal power extended its influence considerably. Thousands who resisted its decrees were put to the sword. The massacre of the Huguenots offers but one example of the Papacy's bloody excesses. Heretics paid a dear price for their desires for freedom and self-expression. Did not John say that this kingdom would persecute? "And it was given unto him to make war with the saints, and to overcome them: and power was given him over all kindreds, and tongues, and nations" (verse 7).

Centuries before John's prophecy, Daniel predicted the rise of the same power, and he designated its work and nature: "And he shall speak great words against the most High, and shall wear out the saints of the most High, and think to change times and laws: and they shall be given into his hand until a time and times and the dividing of time" (Daniel 7:25). The boastful claims of Catholicism for its popes and the privileges granted its bishops and priests exceed the limits of blasphemy. That a religion would exalt any man to equality with Christ is to speak "great words against the most High." But this, Roman Catholicism did. "And meekly stepping to the throne of Caesar, the *Vicar of Christ* took up the sceptre, to which emperors and kings of Europe were to bow in reverence through so many ages" (*American Catholic Quarterly Review,* April, 1911). The reader is appalled at the folly of Henry IV, German emperor, who had to stand barefoot for three days in the snow while he waited for an audience with Pope Gregory VII. Such was the power of the Papacy.

Daniel's prophecy further states that this power would "think to change times and laws." John spoke of the "mark" of the beast. What, indeed, was the mark or sign of Catholic world authority? Notice the Roman Church's own answer.

> Q. *Have you any other way of proving that the Church has power to institute festivals of precept?*
> A. Had she not such power, she could not have done that in which all modern religionists agree with her;—she could not have substituted the observance of Sunday, the first day of the week, for the observance of Saturday, the seventh day, a change for which there is no Scriptural authority" (Stephen Keenan, *A Doctrinal Catechism*, p. 174).

It is interesting that the Papacy borrowed its day of worship from paganism. The law of Constantine, March 7, 321, exempted farmers but enjoined all others to rest "on the venerable day of the sun" (Cod. Just., iii, Tit. 12, 3). Eusebius, who worked closely with Constantine, says, "All things whatsoever that it was the duty to do on the Sabbath, these we have transferred to the Lord's day" (*Commentary on the Psalms*). The Augsburg Confession, Article XXVIII, a Lutheran Protestant document, acknowledges this: "They [the Catholics] appeal to the fact the Sabbath changed to Sunday—contrary, as they say, to the Ten Commandments. No case is appealed to and urged so insistently as the change of the Sabbath, for thereby they wish to maintain that the power of the church is indeed great because the church has dispensed from and altered part of the Ten Commandments" (*Creeds of the Churches*, pp. 100, 101).

That any man or institution would tamper with the Decalogue is utter blasphemy. But history points to the Roman Church as the culprit. The change of the Sabbath is the basis of its claim to universal authority. The acceptance of the man-commanded day and the rejection of the Sabbath of Scripture is the *mark of the beast!* That this mark will be applied at a future crisis in history matters little once we understand that the willful rejection of God's will and the acceptance of a man-originated practice, cannot lessen one's guilt. One's understanding is the key determinant here.

The seventh-day Sabbath is deeply embedded in Creation. "Thus the heavens and the earth were finished, and all the host of them. . . . And God blessed the seventh day, and sanctified it: because that in it he had rested from all his work which God created and made" (Genesis 2:1-3).

Scripture clearly teaches that *Saturday* is the Sabbath day. Mark 15:42 calls the day of the Crucifixion "the day before the sabbath." Sunday is readily identified and universally understood to be the day of the Resurrection. The Bible calls it the first day of the week. "Now when Jesus was risen early the first day of the week, he appeared first to Mary Magdalene, out of whom he had cast seven devils" (Mark 16:9). The women came on this day to anoint Jesus' body, but they were late. He had risen! "Now upon the first day of the week, very early in the morning, they came unto the sepulchre, bringing the spices which they had prepared, and certain others with them" (Luke 24:1). Verse 13 states that two disciples "went that same day" to Emmaus. As they walked along they talked about the Crucifixion. When Jesus joined them, they said, "But we trusted that it had been he which should have redeemed Israel: and beside all this, to day is the third day since these things were done" (verse 21).

If we count back three days from Sunday and include Sunday, we arrive at Friday, the day of the Crucifixion. Friday, according to Mark, is "the day before the sabbath" (15:42).

Saturday is, then, the true Lord's day of Scripture.

"Therefore the Son of man is Lord also of the sabbath" (Mark 2:28). "But the seventh day is the sabbath of the Lord thy God" (Exodus 20:10). "If thou turn away thy foot from the sabbath, from doing thy pleasure on my holy day . . ." (Isaiah 58:13). Saturday was thus the day to which John referred when he said, "I was in the Spirit on the Lord's day" (Revelation 1:10).

Observance of the Sabbath acknowledges God's creative power, according to Exodus 20:11. It also signifies sanctification. "I gave them my sabbaths, to be a sign between me and them, that they might know that I am the Lord that sanctify them" (Ezekiel 20:12).

As I write this chapter I am in the middle of an evangelistic campaign. A young man has just had to confront the choice of losing a good job to keep the Sabbath or of continuing with business as usual. It was an agonizing experience for him, especially in light of the present economic situation. Last night he made his decision. He would obey God rather than man. His countenance radiated his joy as he shook my hand. Although we must often make tough decisions, once we decide the issue in favor of truth, God showers the faithful with His blessings and makes the former mental anguish worthwhile. A God who does not change enjoins the planet to "remember the sabbath day, to keep it holy" (Exodus 20:8).

Most established Protestant bodies have never accepted the Sabbath of the Bible. To their everlasting credit, the founders of the Seventh-day Adventist Church embraced the apostles' day of worship. This church has been foremost in proclaiming the Sabbath truth to the world.

The Buffalo

"And I beheld another beast coming up out of the

earth; and he had two horns like a lamb, and he spake as a dragon" (Revelation 13:11). This second kingdom leads the world "to worship the first beast" (the Papacy), and it imitates the Papacy in punishing dissenters. Moreover, this buffalo enforces the papal Sunday on a nationwide scale—and a wondering world follows suit.

The nation here described represents an America that we do not now know. Roger Williams and many early settlers did, indeed, feel the heavy hand of Protestant persecution in our early history. But he helped change all of this. James Madison and Thomas Jefferson put the capstone on the Constitution by inserting the Bill of Rights, guaranteeing the freedom that we now enjoy. And so for some two hundred years Americans have led the world as champions of civil and religious liberty. The statue of liberty, its lamp shining continuously, beckons the oppressed of many lands to enjoy our grand experiment in human liberty.

But the buffalo spoke like a dragon. Some early expositors applied these words to American slavery, the most brutal in the history of man. The Civil War resulted in the emancipation of slaves in 1865. Yet others view America's courtship of the Papacy, the presence of Sunday laws on the books of the majority of states, and the characterization of those laws as social in nature as paving the way for a crisis to come.

Protestants nationwide are organizing to become a political force in 1980. Their avowed purpose is to influence legislators. Heard again in the land is this threat issued November 20, 1920, by the secretary of the Sunday Law Society: "We shall agitate until no Congressman who cares to stay in Congress will dare refuse to vote for our measures." The move today seeks to rally a "moral majority" that will elect officials who feel sympathetic to conservative Protestant programs. Is memory so short that we would so soon forget the lessons of medieval history? Will this fabled land of wealth and liberty barter its soul for a mess of Protestant pottage? Will our liberties, so dearly bought, be sacrificed on the altar of high-sounding rhetoric?

The United States is not a theocratic government. And in man-administered government, religion and politics don't mix. No emergency is so severe as to justify our tampering with solutions that prostrated Europe. It is too easy, in the name of emergency, to curtail freedoms that are the life of the nation. What day a man worships on is not the state's business. Nor is the relationship enhanced when the church dictates to political officials. Neither panic nor pride should lead us down a road already traveled—to a continent's ruin. But this lesson from the past is buried and largely forgotten, raising the ugly prospect that a generation far removed from 1777 might repeat the mistakes of the past.

The prophets have spoken. The verdict is in. The sword will be unsheathed. Inquisitions will be revived. Heretics, at least the fortunate ones, will take to the hills. Their property will be confiscated. The saints will be hated. Ministers will be imprisoned and forgotten. Torture will be used to extract confessions. The Seer of Patmos has spoken. The latter-day prophet, Ellen G. White, has backed him up.

Those who believe the prophets await the time and circumstance.

Chapter 13

Crossing Over!

Israel had wandered in the wilderness for forty years. Behind them lay many battles fought and won. They had been confined to this sunbaked wilderness until a generation would die out. These complainers had taxed God's tolerance with their rebellion. At last the sentence of death had been executed. Their bones were bleaching on the sands of the wilderness. Even Moses could only view the Land of Promise before his burial on the mountain.

But now their sons and daughters could cross over Jordan. With Caleb and Joshua at its head, a vast army of young Israelites surged toward the river Jordan. The river parted before them, and they joyously crossed on dry land. They had reached the "land . . . [of] milk and honey," a land that would forever be identified with the children of Israel. This was the land of their fathers' dreams. Of this they had whispered quietly during the long night of Egyptian slavery. They had dreamed of a better day for their children—and it was here at last!

The church of the living God has wandered long in this wilderness of sin. Her trek to the Promised Land began long ago with the calling of the Twelve. Through resistance from Judaism and because of pagan and papal persecutions the church has left a bloody trail to the water's edge. The remnant church (visible) is the last church of history. It stands on the threshold of the kingdom of God. The signs of the end pictured in Matthew 24 and Luke 21 are fast fulfilling. The prophecies of Daniel 2 and Daniel 7 are near historic termination. "The times of the Gentiles" are nearly fulfilled. Man's stay on this planet is now threatened by God's timetable. The sands in the hourglass are almost spent. This is, indeed, the time of the end.

Spiritual declension is everywhere evident. Long ere this, form replaced divine power in the lives of multitudes. A mysterious lethargy has paralyzed thousands on the eve of Armageddon. Creature comforts play their part, but the malady lies deeper. The small percentage of Christians who engage in personal mission outreach says that few people feel deeply for a lost world. This is not a harsh personal judgment. It is the tragic truth.

In the multiple tragedies that daily stalk humanity, God speaks not only to the world but to the church. Volcanic eruptions, the Cambodian tragedy, and the devastation of populated areas by tornadoes, typhoons, and hurricanes all sound their ominous warnings of worse things to come. But through it all the world and many church members seem oblivious to its deep significance. The truth is, sin has so aged the earth that its chemistry has been altered. Nature itself is no longer stable. The weather is cold when it should be hot, and hot when and where it should be cold. Scientists have detected a significant movement of the polar ice cap. The sun seems hotter, indicating to some that we in our nuclear experimentation just may have tampered with the ozone layer. In short, the planet itself is rapidly becoming unfit for human habitation.

It is clear that we face a climactic resolution of the sin problem. An event both dreadful and glorious presses itself upon us. Signs of the approaching end have accelerated both in frequency and intensity. The Bible predicted deteriorating human relations during these times. Violence stalks the streets. There is little safety for life or property. Add to all of this the unsettled state of international affairs, and the immediate future of the human family is not very bright.

What will arouse the sleeping saints from their Laodicean slumber? Our minds have been conditioned to tragedy by the daily assaults of the media. We have been fed the shocking so often and for so long that our minds have become desensitized. Perhaps some ultimate tragedy awaits us. Could it be that we will awaken one day to find our spiritual privileges severely curtailed? Is there a planetwide persecution of the remnant church in our future? It just may be that this alone can arouse the great majority of saints to desperate action in reaching the unsaved.

"And at that time shall Michael stand up, the great prince which standeth for the children of thy people: and there shall be a time of trouble, such as never was since there was a nation even to that same time: and at that time thy people shall be delivered, every one that shall be found written in the book" (Daniel 12:1). In the early stages of this trouble, prior to the standing up of Michael, it seems that there will be a great shaking in the ranks of the remnant. Those who have not anchored their souls (Hebrews 6:19) through daily dependence upon God, prayer, Bible study, and Christian service will be shaken out, while thousands who have read and heard God's truth will be gathered in.

Then "they that be wise shall shine as the brightness of the firmament; and they that turn many to righteousness as the stars for ever and ever" (Daniel 12:3). Daniel here speaks of unlimited missionary activity. Thousands of saints will awaken to their own as well as to the needs of others. They will press from door to door with the soul-saving messages of Revelation 14. This missionary movement will be worldwide in scope. The church will in that day be "fair as the moon, clear as the sun, and terrible as an army with banners" (Song of Solomon 6:10).

After the great revival, Michael will stand up. Christ will have ended His final work in behalf of man. At that time the work of mediation, substitution, intercession, and investigative judgment will be over. We will then see sinners in the hands of an angry God. The plagues of Revelation 16 will fall upon the people. Just as in ancient Egypt ten plagues paved the way for the Exodus, so in the last days seven plagues will precede the remnant's "crossing over."

Under the first plague "there fell a noisome and grievous sore upon the men which had the mark of the beast, and upon them which worshipped his image" (Revelation 16:2). Under the second plague "the sea . . . became as the blood of a dead man: and every living soul died in the sea" (verse 3). "And the third angel poured out his vial upon the rivers and fountains of waters; and they became blood" (verse 4). Under the fourth plague the sun was given power "to scorch men with fire" (verse 8). The seat of the beast is the target of the fifth plague: "And his kingdom was full of darkness; and they gnawed their tongues for pain" (verse 10). The sixth plague is Armageddon—the end of the world.

"Behold, I come as a thief. Blessed is he that watcheth, and keepeth his garments, lest he walk naked, and they see his shame" (Revelation 16:15). "And, behold, I come quickly; and my reward is with me, to give every man according as his work shall be" (Revelation 22:12). Again and again Scripture brings us back to the Second Coming. The Hope of the human race is on His way. The remnant church will be torn from this doomed planet.

The seventh plague, the plague of hail, will be so

violent that each hailstone will weigh almost a talent (over fifty pounds). Man's reaction to this plague is also violent, because the Bible says, "Men blasphemed God because of the plague of the hail; for the plague thereof was exceeding great" (Revelation 16:21). God the Father and all of the angels will empty heaven as they accompany the Son in His triumphal reentry to this planet.

The king of Buganda, His Majesty Mutesa II, had been exiled to England. Many months of negotiations were necessary to effect his return. I was in that country for three months during his absence. Every Buganda heart felt heavy, for in a real sense the king is the head of every home. The people waited in prayerful hope of their monarch's early return. Psychologically, a part of every citizen was in London.

As time went on, the Buganda people grew sullen. They began to boycott foreign-owned businesses. Church attendance fell off. Life slowed down to a crawl. The mood turned hostile. So the colonial governor was recalled. The decision was made in London—the king would return.

Thousands gathered at the airport at Entebbe. Still other thousands lined the highway from Entebbe to Kampala. Soon the roar of the aircraft was heard, and British fighter craft, dipping their wings, flew over the airport. The crowd roared in anticipation. Soon the plane bearing their king glided onto the runway. The thousands of people waved banana palms in greeting as young Mutesa rode in triumph to his throne thirty miles away.

Soon the King of kings and Lord of lords will make His glorious appearance in the clouds. His promise, made so long ago, will be fulfilled. He will appear in awesome splendor to millions of His waiting people. "Lo, this is our God; we have waited for him, and he will save us" (Isaiah 25:9), the expectant millions will chant. Mountains will

be moved out of their places, and islands will disappear.
The planet will sway in its orbit like the uncertain gait of
a drunkard. All that is man-made will be ground to pow-
der, and the wind will blow it away as the chaff from
"summer threshingfloors." The wicked will be struck
dead at the brightness of His coming (2 Thessalonians
2:8). "The dead in Christ shall rise first" (1 Thessalonians
4:16). The righteous dead will join the righteous living as
they are caught away to God (1 Thessalonians 4:17). But
both will be changed in a moment, in the twinkling of an
eye (1 Corinthians 15:51-54).

These cataclysmic events do not disturb the wicked,
because they will sleep for a thousand years (Revelation
20:5). During those thousand years the saints shall judge
the world (Revelation 20:4). The devil will be confined to
this desolated earth (verses 1, 2). He will be given one
thousand years to prove his original contention that he is
a god and should, therefore, be included in the council on
Creation. But in one thousand years it will be seen that
he cannot create a solitary, living thing. The universe
will look on in amazement at his frustrated attempts. At
the end of the millennium he will stand unmasked as the
impostor that he is. Only the wicked dead will remain
unaware of his *true nature*.

At the end of the thousand years the Holy City will
descend (Revelation 21:2). The wicked dead will be raised
(Revelation 20:5). Satan will rally them for one last abor-
tive struggle with God (verse 8). But God will destroy
them by fire (verses 9, 10). Everything on this planet will
be burned up (Malachi 4:1; 2 Peter 3:10, 11). Affliction
will not rise again a second time (Nahum 1:9).

Christ will then step forth to re-create the earth into a
thing of beauty. "Behold, I make all things new" (Revelation 21:5), He says. "For, behold, I create new heavens
and a new earth: and the former shall not be remembered,

nor come into mind" (Isaiah 65:17). There will be no rental property. Every man will sit under his own vine and fig tree (Micah 4:4). There will be no more war, death, pain, or sickness. "And God shall wipe away all tears from their eyes; and there shall be no more death, neither sorrow, nor crying, neither shall there be any more pain: for the former things are passed away" (Revelation 21:4). No longer to have to contend with the former things will be heaven enough!

The city of God will rest in that day on the Mount of Olives (Zechariah 14:4). The joyous cry will be heard in the land, "Behold, the tabernacle of God is with men, and he will dwell with them, and they shall be his people, and God himself shall be with them, and be their God" (Revelation 21:3). The long exodus will be over. The saints, amid fragrant flowers and plunging waterfalls, will bask in the sunlight of God's favor. World without end. Amen!